THE
THIN BOOK
OF TRUST

An Essential Primer for Building Trust at Work

Third Edition

CHARLES FELTMAN

Berrett–Koehler Publishers, Inc.

Berrett-Koehler Publishers, Inc.
1333 Broadway, Suite P100
Oakland, CA 94612-1921
Tel: (510) 817-2277
Fax: (510) 817-2278
bkconnection.com

ORDERING INFORMATION
Quantity sales. Special discounts are available on quantity purchases by corporations, associations, and others. For details, please go to bkconnection.com to see our bulk discounts or contact bookorders@bkpub.com for more information.
Individual sales. Berrett-Koehler publications are available through most bookstores. They can also be ordered directly from Berrett-Koehler: Tel: (800) 929-2929; Fax: (802) 864-7626; bkconnection.com.
Orders for college textbook / course adoption use. Please contact Berrett-Koehler: Tel: (800) 929-2929; Fax: (802) 864-7626.

Distributed to the US trade and internationally by Penguin Random House Publisher Services.

Berrett-Koehler and the BK logo are registered trademarks of Berrett-Koehler Publishers, Inc.

Printed in the United States of America

Berrett-Koehler books are printed on long-lasting acid-free paper. When it is available, we choose paper that has been manufactured by environmentally responsible processes. These may include using trees grown in sustainable forests, incorporating recycled paper, minimizing chlorine in bleaching, or recycling the energy produced at the paper mill.

Library of Congress Cataloging-in-Publication Data

Names: Feltman, Charles, author.
Title: The thin book of trust : an essential primer for building trust at work / Charles Feltman.
Description: Third edition. | Oakland, CA : Berrett-Koehler Publishers, Inc., [2024] | Includes bibliographical references and index.
Identifiers: LCCN 2024010385 (print) | LCCN 2024010386 (ebook) | ISBN 9798890570390 (paperback) | ISBN 9798890570406 (pdf) | ISBN 9798890570413 (epub)
Subjects: LCSH: Honesty in the workplace. | Trust. | Management—Moral and ethical aspects. | Work environment.
Classification: LCC HF5549.5.H66 F45 2024 (print) | LCC HF5549.5.H66 (ebook) | DDC 174/.4—dc23/eng/20240501
LC record available at https://lccn.loc.gov/2024010385
LC ebook record available at https://lccn.loc.gov/2024010386

Third Edition
32 31 30 29 28 27 26 25 24   10 9 8 7 6 5
Book producer: PeopleSpeak
Text designer: Reider Books
Cover designer: Ashley Ingram

To my wife and life partner, Laura Cooper, whose trust, support, and encouragement allow me to constantly push my imagined boundaries. To Ila Edgar, my trusted thinking partner in exploring trust in all its forms. To my clients, for their treasured trust in me and from whom I've learned much of what I know about building trust.

Contents

Preface to the Third Edition

As I write this preface for the third edition of *The Thin Book of Trust*, this book has sold close to one hundred thousand copies. That isn't a big number for many books, but for a slim volume that has had no marketing, it is a big accomplishment. It has found an appreciative audience of leaders, managers, coaches, consultants, facilitators, boards, church congregations, school districts, and many others who have used it to strengthen, sustain, and sometimes repair trust in their individual and collective relationships. It has done so based on the value of what it offers: a clear, concise, effective framework and set of practices for building trust.

I've often been asked how I got interested in this work and what brought me to write the book. In my twenty years of working in organizations and twenty-five more coaching and developing leaders, two truths became clear to me. The first is that trust truly is the foundation for both success and well-being at work, and the ability to build, maintain, and repair it is a mission-critical leadership competency. The second is that having a clear, powerful, accessible trust framework makes developing and strengthening that competency significantly easier and faster.

If you are opening this book for the first time, congratulations. You are starting on a journey to becoming an exceptional trust builder in your workplace. If you are a longtime fan of the book and have purchased the third edition to see what's new, I trust you will find something valuable in it that will add to what your first reading gave you, further increasing your ability in this critical competency.

My intention with this book and all the work I do in the field of trust building is to help people create a strong foundation of trust that will support greater success, well-being, joy, and even love for the work they do and those they do it with. My hope is that you, dear reader, become a master trust builder, able to consistently build trust up, down, and across your organization. In doing so you will help bring greater success and well-being to everyone you work with. You will also be an example to others to become master trust builders, and so the trust circle grows.

INTRODUCTION

Trust in the Work Environment

We're never so vulnerable than when we trust someone—but paradoxically, if we cannot trust, neither can we find love or joy.

—Walter Anderson

This is a small book about a very important subject. A lot has been written about trust: about what it is and what it can do for people, families, companies, communities, and countries. As an executive coach and consultant, I often find myself engaged by companies where good work is being sabotaged by interpersonal conflict, political infighting, paralysis, stagnation, apathy, or cynicism. I almost always trace these problems to a breakdown in trust. This not only kills good work, it also inevitably creates some degree of misery, annoyance, fear, anger, frustration, resentment, and resignation. By contrast, in successful companies where people are innovative, engage in productive conflict and debate about ideas, and have fun working together, I find strong, trusting relationships. As a result, I've come to believe having the trust of those you work with is too important to not be intentional about building and maintaining it.

With this book, you will learn how to build and maintain strong, trusting relationships with others and repair trust when it is broken by being intentional and consistent in your language and actions. Understanding and consistently demonstrating trustworthy language and behavior will help you earn and keep the trust of the people you work with.

ASSESS THE ENVIRONMENT

My colleagues and I asked the following questions in a survey where, on a scale of 1 to 10, 10 equals "can always be trusted in all situations" and 1 equals "can rarely or never be trusted."

- How would you rate your own trustworthiness?
- How would you rate the trustworthiness of your coworkers?
- How would you rate your immediate supervisor?
- How would you rate your company's top management?

Respondents gave the following ratings on average:

- Their own trustworthiness: 8.72
- Their coworkers': 7.59
- Their immediate supervisors': 8.33
- Their company's top management's: 6.43

The results indicate that we generally judge others to be less trustworthy than ourselves. If most of the people you work with are also like our survey respondents, they are making the same judgments. That means some of the people you work with likely judge you to be less trustworthy than you consider yourself to be. Your first thought may be that they are mistaken. Certainly you don't intend to act in ways others view as untrustworthy, so they must be misinterpreting your intentions. But the fact is people act on their assessments of your trustworthiness, not your own estimation. Your best intentions can't change their opinion. Only changing what you say and how you act can affect how others assess your trustworthiness.

Most people say that having the trust of others helps get good work done. But if you ask how they build and maintain trust with others, their answers are often simplistic. Even people who consistently maintain strong trust relationships with those around them will say, "I keep my commitments" or "I tell the truth and expect others to do the same" or "I try to let people know I care about them." However, it may not be clear how others actually assess their trustworthiness.

In addition to not clearly knowing how others assess trustworthiness, people face many and often conflicting demands on their time and attention at work. Priorities change frequently, sometimes in a matter of minutes. There isn't enough time to get everything done. So while you may try to be honest, keep your commitments, and show others you care about them, the environment of your organization may make it difficult for you to do so. In addition, recognition and compensation structures may encourage the kind of competition that damages trust between people. Divisions, departments, or teams may exist in silos that tend to cultivate distrust. With so many factors outside of your control, where can you as an individual begin?

FRAMEWORK FOR TRUST

This book offers a framework for the following topics related to trust:

- Developing and sustaining others' trust in you by intentionally speaking and acting in ways that other people consider to be trustworthy, even in today's fast-paced, demanding, and constantly changing work environments
- Talking constructively with people about distrust when you need to
- Restoring trust with others when it has been broken
- Making wise choices about when and to what extent you trust others

Trust is critical for everyone who wants to work with others to accomplish what is not possible to do alone. The great news is that building trust is a competency, a set of skills that can be learned and improved. This means no matter how good you are at it now, you can get even better. You will find that the ability to consistently build and maintain trust enhances everything else you do. This book is intended as a primer for improving your ability to increase trust with your employees, colleagues, boss, customers, suppliers, and other important stakeholders. What you take from this little book can even spill over into your family and community life.

WHAT IS TRUST?

Both popular and scientific literature explore the many different models and definitions of trust. However, the focus of this book is to help people learn to more consistently build and maintain trust at work. For this purpose, trust is defined as *choosing to risk making something you value vulnerable to another person's actions.*

When you trust someone, what you make vulnerable can range from concrete rewards, such as money, a job, a promotion, or a particular goal, to less tangible values, such as a belief you hold, a cherished way of doing things, your good name, or even your sense of happiness and well-being. Whatever you choose to make vulnerable to another's actions, you do so because you believe you and they will accomplish something worthwhile together that you couldn't alone and that their actions will support or, at the very least, will not harm what you have made vulnerable.

Some people extend trust to others easily and with little or no evidence that it is warranted. They withdraw their trust only if it is betrayed. Others believe that people must earn their trust by demonstrating trustworthiness. Whether you tend to trust more or less easily, you do so by assessing the probability that the other person will support or harm what you value in the future. In this sense choosing to trust or distrust is a risk assessment.

BUILDING TRUST IS A TWO-WAY STREET

Building trust requires being trustworthy and trusting wisely. You may be highly trustworthy, but if you don't extend trust to others, none is built. I have worked with managers and leaders who are mystified that trust is low in their teams, departments, or companies. But a closer look often reveals that the problem starts with the leader's lack of trust in the people who work for and with them.

Applying the framework described in this book will help you strengthen trust in both directions: making wise choices about when and to what extent you trust others and consistently showing up as a trustworthy person yourself. This, in turn, will contribute to building and maintaining trust with other individuals, on teams, and throughout your organization.

> ☑ **TRUST CHECK**
>
> Think of someone you trust and consider these questions:
>
> - What is it you are willing to entrust to them that you consider valuable?
> - Why do you trust them with this?
> - How do you demonstrate that trust?
> - What do the people you work with entrust to you?
> - Why do you think they trust you?

KEY DISTINCTIONS

The choice to trust consists of four distinct assessments about how someone is likely to act. These assessments are *care, sincerity, reliability,* and *competence.* Together they define what we consider to be a person's trustworthiness. Through the assessment of these attributes, you can clearly identify what may be getting in the way of trusting others. For example, someone may be competent or able to do the work but is not reliable. You can address the reliability issue with this person rather than simply labeling them as untrustworthy. This process also works in understanding how others judge your trustworthiness.

TRUST AND DISTRUST

It is difficult to talk about trust without addressing distrust and its consequences. Distrust is essentially the opposite of trust in that it is a choice to not make yourself vulnerable to another person's actions. It is an assessment that tells you what is important to you is not safe with this person in this situation (or any situation). This could include the work you or your team are doing, a deadline you need to meet, your reputation or status, or your health or happiness. Whatever it is, distrust reflects your fear that the person will mishandle, damage, lose, destroy, steal, or use it for their gain. When you distrust another person, you look for ways to protect what you value. The disaster of distrust in the workplace is that the strategies people use to protect themselves inevitably get in the way of their ability to effectively work with others.

For example, if I start protecting myself, the strategies I typically use—resistance, withholding, avoiding, arguing, ignoring, or directly attacking—are guaranteed to produce or intensify the other person's distrust of me. Thus we spiral down into deeper distrust. Meanwhile, others around us may begin to distrust one or both of us as well. Table 1 compares trust and distrust in terms of how people think, feel, and behave and some of what is going on in their brains and nervous systems. The good news is that we can take constructive action when we distrust someone by using more precise language, something beyond simply saying, "I don't trust you." I'll cover more about distrust in chapter 6.

First, I'm going to provide an overview of the four distinctions of trust—care, sincerity, reliability, and competence. Chapter 6 will focus on how to talk productively with others about why you distrust them and how that can be changed. Chapter 7 is a primer on how you can repair trust when you have broken it. Chapter 8 takes a high-level look at the neuroscience of trust and how understanding it can be useful in building it. Chapter 9 focuses on the aspects of trust building that are unique to teams. I end the book with a chapter on starting your practice of intentionally building trust by using the framework and language from the book.

Table 1. Trust and distrust in ourselves and others

	Trust	Distrust
Assessments about another person	• I can trust this person. • I am safe with this person.	• It is dangerous to trust this person. • This person poses a threat to me.
Assessments about myself	• I am safe. • I can handle whatever happens. • I can be open and forthcoming.	• I am not safe. • I can't handle what this person might do. • I need to protect myself.
Associated emotions	• Acceptance, safety, curiosity, generosity, hope, care	• Fear, anger, resentment, resignation, cynicism
Behaviors	• Cooperating, collaborating, talking about and debating ideas, listening, communicating freely, supporting others, sharing information, offering ideas, expecting the best, giving the benefit of the doubt, being willing to examine my own actions	• Defending, resisting, blaming, complaining, judging, avoiding, withholding information and ideas, expecting the worst, justifying protective actions based on distrust
Neuro-physiology	• Normal to elevated levels of oxytocin • Full availability of neocortex (the "thinking brain") and limbic system brain structures to make decisions and take action • Ability to intervene in and change preprogrammed neural patterns	• Priming of the brain's primary defense systems for any sign of imminent danger • Elevated levels of adrenaline, cortisol, and other fight, flight, or freeze hormones and neurotransmitters • Limited use of neocortex, greater reliance on defense-related, preprogrammed neural patterns for making decisions and taking action

☑ TRUST CHECK

Reflect on your own patterns of trust:

- If a new employee in your company asked your manager how trustworthy you are, what do you think they would say?
- If this person asked your peers, what would they likely say?
- When you do not yet have any experience with how someone behaves, what is your usual attitude toward trusting them?
- Are there certain types or categories of people you tend to trust more or less? If so, what are those types?
- What criteria do you use to decide how far to trust someone when you don't know anything about them?

TAKE THE TRUST SURVEY YOURSELF

Take the trust survey below. Use a scale of 1 to 10, where 10 means the person or people can always be trusted in all situations and 1 means they can rarely or never be trusted.

1. Rate your own trustworthiness.
2. Rate the average trustworthiness of the people you work with as a group.
3. Rate the trustworthiness of your immediate supervisor.
4. Rate the trustworthiness of your company's top management in general.
5. Rate the trustworthiness of your peers in the company.

6. Rate the trustworthiness of your direct reports. (If you do not manage anyone, leave this question blank.)
7. Rate the trustworthiness of others below your level of responsibility in your company as a group.

Compare your responses to the average ratings at the beginning of the chapter. Are yours similar? What might this tell you about trust in your work environment? As we take a deeper look at the trust framework, consider what you can do to help those you work with become more trustworthy.

CHAPTER 1

The Language of Trust

Trust is the stacking and layering of small moments and reciprocal vulnerability over time.

—Brené Brown

Trust is fundamental to our sense of safety, autonomy, and dignity as human beings. It is also an integral part of every relationship we have. When we trust someone, we feel safe to share what is important to us, including our thoughts, ideas, efforts, hopes, and concerns. When others trust us, they reciprocate in kind. It doesn't mean we always agree, just that we listen to, respect, and value what each other has to offer. In fact, trust allows us to disagree, debate, and test each other's thinking as we work together to find the best ideas and solutions. Having work relationships built on trust allows us to get better and faster results with less stress.

Consider the following two examples of people talking about their leaders, Randy and Ray.

Randy is in charge of information systems for a midsize service company. Anita reports to Randy, along with three other managers, and each of them manages several other people. This is how Anita describes her relationship with Randy:

I have a great working relationship with Randy. Even though Randy is our boss, the five of us work as a team most of the time. We get a lot done and have a good time doing it. And it shows because our clients often tell us they appreciate what we do for them, which makes me proud to be part of this organization.

We don't always agree, and Randy does have the final say, but he'll always hear each of us out before he makes a decision. He makes his share of mistakes, of course, just like the rest of us. But we each take responsibility for them when we do, and we try to learn from them. Another thing that is important to me is that Randy also checks his facts before he says something, and his opinions are based on evidence, which he shares with us.

The bottom line is I trust Randy. I trust he knows what he's doing and has what's good for our clients and the company foremost in mind. He's not one of these people who's all good intentions but never follows through. He does what he says he'll do. He is direct and doesn't beat around the bush. If I'm doing something wrong, or he thinks I'm not doing my best work, he won't hesitate to talk to me about it. But he is also quick to tell me when he thinks I'm doing something well. And I know both are for the sake of my professional growth and development.

In contrast, here is what Lisa has to say about her boss, Ray. Lisa and three other coworkers report to Ray. They are supposed to work as a team to process loans.

Our office has the lowest productivity in the region, and it's because of Ray. To be honest, I don't think the man knows what he's doing most of the time, but he won't admit it or ask anyone how to do things right. Instead he makes mistakes and then blames someone else when his mistakes cause problems, which they always do. The someone who gets blamed is usually one of us loan processors. I've even caught him in outright lies he's told to cover for mistakes he made. If I see he's about to do something that isn't to regulations and tell him about it, does he thank me for it? No. Instead he argues with me about it, like he knows what he's talking about, until I show him the specific regulation or procedure.

Not only do I not trust that he knows what he's doing on the loans, I'm sure he's bad-mouthing me and the other people here to his boss and our customers to make it sound like we're the ones who are messing up. I don't even talk to the man anymore unless I absolutely have to. And it's too bad because it's the customers who ultimately suffer.

The working relationships fostered by Randy and Ray were vastly different. In one, manager and employee built trust together; the other dissolved into distrust. Over time, in both situations the link between words and actions determined the trust relationship. Randy was aware of the importance of his language and actions in building and maintaining trust. More importantly, he understood the fundamental language of trust, the distinctions of care, sincerity, reliability, and competence that people use to think about and judge his trustworthiness. Just as important, Randy had a high degree of trust in the people on his team as well. This trust was a two-way street that benefited everyone.

Ray, on the other hand, consistently failed to appreciate the connection between what he said and what he did and how the disconnect created distrust. Nor did he have any idea why people were judging him as untrustworthy. As a result, he created

---

✔️ TRUST CHECK

Take a moment to reflect on Randy's and Ray's situations:

- What is the general mood and attitude toward work on Randy's team?
- What about on Ray's team?
- If you were Ray's peer and had the opportunity to give him three suggestions for how to build trust with his employees, what would they be?

---

enormous distrust in his workplace. Not only did his staff, supervisors, and clients distrust him, but also he distrusted them. While it began with Ray, everyone in and around that office behaved in such a way that no one felt they could fully trust anyone else.

Both Anita and Lisa have made a choice, a decision to trust or not trust. Figure 1 shows a model of trust as a decision.

When Anita said, "I trust Randy," she was actually making an overall judgment that includes all four distinctions. For example, when she said, "He does what he says he'll do," she was talking about her assessment of his sincerity and reliability. Her statement "Randy checks his facts before he says something, and his opinions are based on evidence, which he shares with us" also indicated her judgment of his sincerity. When she said, "I trust he knows what he's doing and has what's good for our clients and the company foremost in mind," she was talking about his competence and the care she believed he held toward what she also valued. Taken together, the four assessments combined to add up to her trust in him.

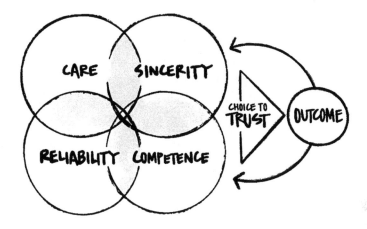

Figure 1. Choice to trust model

Anita was not alone in her strong trust of her manager. Randy's other direct reports, his peers, and his manager all expressed similarly high levels of trust in him. As Anita's description attests, the strong trust that Randy evoked in the people around him was good for him, good for them, and good for the company they worked in.

Ray's behavior, on the other hand, left his staff, supervisors, and clients to distrust him. As Lisa pointed out, their office was the least productive in their region. All of them, Ray included, were spending so much time, energy, and creativity defending themselves against what they feared others would do or try to do to them that they had little to spare for their real work.

THE DISTINCTIONS

The following four distinctions compose a framework for understanding how you assess other peoples' trustworthiness and how they assess yours.

Care is the assessment that you have the other person's interests in mind as well as your own when you make decisions and take actions. Of the four assessments of trustworthiness, care is in some ways the most important for building lasting trust. When people believe you are concerned with only your self-interest and don't consider their interests as well, they may trust your sincerity, reliability, and competence, but they will tend to limit their trust of you to specific situations or transactions. On the other hand, when people believe you hold their interests in mind, they will extend their trust more broadly to you.

Sincerity is the assessment that you are honest, that you say what you mean and mean what you say. You can be believed and taken seriously. It also means your opinions are seen as valid, useful, and backed up by sound thinking and evidence. Finally, it means that your actions will align with your words.

Reliability is the assessment that you meet the commitments you make, that you keep your promises. Keeping promises is another way of saying you'll follow through.

Competence is the assessment that you have the ability to do what you are doing or propose to do. In the workplace this usually means others believe you have the requisite capacity, skill, knowledge, and resources to do a particular task or job.

TRUST IS NOT ALL OR NOTHING

Understanding trust as a collection of assessments in four different domains frees us from the limiting belief that trust is all or nothing. We can be wiser and more precise about extending trust.

You can, for example, determine someone is not trustworthy in the domain of reliability because he often misses deadlines he has agreed to, but you may still be able to trust that he is sincere, is competent in his area of expertise, and cares. Rather than distrusting him completely, which will surely make your work and his more difficult, you can take measures to deal with his failing in the domain of reliability and still benefit from his work in other ways. Or, as I'll discuss later in the book, you can have a conversation with him about your concern with his reliability.

One thing that made the situation worse for Ray and his group was that they all believed either you trust someone fully or not at all. Once Lisa decided she didn't trust Ray in one situation, she figured she couldn't trust anything he did. In fact, she did something most of us unconsciously do: she started looking for other things he did that would further support her judgment he was not trustworthy and ignoring anything that would contradict that judgment, something psychologists call *confirmation bias*. Knowing trust can be assessed in four distinct domains is an antidote to the tendency to engage in confirmation bias. We can more easily step back and ask ourselves whether the other person might be trustworthy in some ways and not others.

As we will see in chapter 7, the four assessment domains give us a better way to talk about and repair broken trust. In the next four chapters we'll look at each distinction of trust in greater depth by reviewing the following:

- What the distinctions mean and how people use each to assess your trustworthiness
- How you can consciously speak and act to build others' trust based on the distinctions
- How these distinctions can be used by teams to build, strengthen, and, if necessary, repair trust

CHAPTER 2

Care

We're in this together

The leaders who work most effectively, it seems to me, never say "I." And that's not because they have trained themselves not to say "I." They don't think "I." They think "we"; they think "team." They understand their job is to make the team function. They accept responsibility and don't sidestep it, but "we" gets the credit. . . . This is what creates trust, what enables you to get the task done.

—Peter Drucker

Care is the assessment you make about the extent to which another person considers your interests and concerns. Another aspect of care is your trust that the other person's intentions toward you are positive, that they want good for you. Of the four assessments of trust, care is in some ways the most important for building lasting trust. When people believe you are concerned with only your self-interest and don't consider their interests as well, they may trust your sincerity, reliability, and competence, but they will limit their trust of you to specific situations or transactions. On the other hand, when people believe you hold their interests in mind and intend good for them, they will extend their trust to you more broadly.

At work, care may mean you are considerate of the interests of an individual or a group to which you belong, such as a team, a department, or the company as a whole. As a leader you can be trusted because even though you may not be able to act in each individual employee's best interests, they believe you are acting in the best interests of the group's shared enterprise. They see your actions as supporting and sustaining what they value. Here are three ways clients of mine have referred to care:

- "One of the things I appreciate about working here is that I know my boss really cares about my professional development. He genuinely wants me to be a capable leader, whether I use those skills here or somewhere else."

- "Getting this product out the door has been a long and winding road, and we wouldn't have made it if our VP hadn't gone to bat for us a few times. There were some heavy hitters in the company who didn't think this was the right product for us, it was costing too much, taking too much time, whatever. But [my boss] cared about getting this thing done, and done right, as much as we did. He may have other shortcomings, but it's great to be working for someone who really cares about what we're working on."

- "We pretty much suspected all along that Bill, our general manager, didn't care about anyone but himself. Last week he made that crystal clear, although I don't think he intended to. We were in a meeting to decide what to do about a major development project that is way behind schedule. At one point Bill came in to have a little chat with us. He probably intended it to be a pep talk. He told us he needed us to work on this 24/7 if that's what it was going to take. Then he actually said, 'If you guys don't get this thing back on track in the next month, I'll be out of a job.' When he left the room, I know everyone around the table was thinking, 'Aha, now we know how to get rid of him.'"

In the example from chapter 1, when Anita talked about how her boss, Randy, points out both her mistakes and what she does well, she said, "I know both are for the sake of my professional growth and development." As she worked with Randy over time, she came to believe that he holds her interests and those of their company at least as high as his own self-interest. If she didn't, even though she saw him as reliable, sincere, and competent, she would probably not be nearly as willing to trust him as much as she does.

LIMITED TRUST

When people believe you have their interests in mind as well as your own, or at least some shared interest, such as that of the team, they will generally extend you their trust with few conditions across many different circumstances. If they do not believe you have their interests or some common interest in mind, many people will simply consider you untrustworthy across all the assessments of sincerity, reliability, and competence. At best they will put conditions on trusting you and limit their trust to specific transactions. You've probably heard someone say something like "I'll work with the guy, but I don't trust him any further than I can throw him." This is one way people talk about someone they believe doesn't care about them. In practice, such a statement could have any of the following meanings:

- "I may be able to believe what he says."
- "She may do what she commits to."
- "He may be competent. However..."
- "I won't trust her to do anything beyond the transaction we are working on now."
- "I won't let him get close to me or know what I'm thinking."
- "I won't share what I care about with her."

Such thinking is usually not explicit either. People certainly won't tell you this is what they think. Moreover, they probably aren't even consciously aware they are thinking this way unless someone asks them directly. They simply act in the unconscious, habitual ways they've developed to protect what is important to them.

CONDITIONAL TRUST

Having someone's limited and conditional trust is better than having them distrust you, but that also means you have to negotiate each transaction. For example, a procurement manager may believe that a salesperson representing a vendor is interested in only what she can gain for herself or her company. He may still be willing to buy products from her, but only because both parties have a legally binding contract to fall back on in case things go wrong, not because he believes the salesperson can be trusted to hold both their interests in mind. As long as nothing goes wrong, it works. But such a limited, conditional trust does not serve people who need to work together effectively for their mutual success.

When some team members believe that others don't care about the collective interests, collaboration deteriorates. Team members can become disengaged or resistant. Interpersonal conflict—overt or covert—increases while healthy exchange and debate of ideas fades. And people begin to distrust their team-mates' sincerity, reliability, and even competence.

A VP who leads a struggling management team recently told me he thought his team's biggest problem was that people weren't completely clear about each other's roles. As an example, he described how a regional director flew to the company's headquarters office to personally represent his region in annual budget meetings. The regional director said it was the operations director's job to represent the region's interests, but apparently the regional director wasn't sure that this would happen. When I later asked the regional director about it, he said he understood the role, he just didn't trust the operations director to fairly represent his region's needs in the meetings.

When people see that you care about them or what they also care about, you don't have to convince them every time you need their trust. And they tend to be more forgiving when things do go wrong. When you occasionally miss a deadline (reliability), say something to one person that contradicts something you said to someone else (sincerity), or make a mistake in your work (competence), others will give you the benefit of the doubt much more readily if they believe you care.

BUILDING TRUST: CARE

Here are some steps you can take to cultivate trust in terms of care:

- Some degree of intimacy is fundamental to the assessment of care in a relationship. Think of the people you believe have your interests at heart. In every case, I bet they have honestly shared with you some of what is important to

☑ TRUST CHECK

Think about your own situation at work and answer these questions:

- Do you believe your supervisor has your interests in mind as well as their own?
- If you manage others, to what extent do you have their interests in mind as well as your own interests? How do you let them know this?
- If you are on a team, do your teammates have the interests of the team at heart when they are doing their work?
- Do you hold the team's interests at heart? How do you let your teammates know?
- When you feel someone doesn't have the best interests of you, your team, group, or company at heart, what effect does it have on you or your work?

them—their values, hopes, dreams, and concerns. This is how intimacy is established and grows. If you want people to believe you are concerned about their interests, listen to what is important to them, and tell them what is important to you.
- Listen to what others say and are trying to communicate. You may have known someone who listened to you as if you were the only person in the world, who gave you their complete attention when you spoke. They let you say what you had to say and didn't respond with words of judgment. They probably also looked you in the eye and may have

asked questions and responded in ways that told you they heard what you meant to say. If you can be this kind of listener for others, they will trust that you care.

- Before you speak or act, ask yourself these questions: Will what I am about to say or do serve the people I work with or for—my employees, teammates, and company—as well as me? Why do I believe it will serve them? If you recognize that what you are thinking of doing is going to serve only yourself and could damage the interests of others, ask yourself if doing it is important enough to risk losing their trust.

- Ask the people you work with what their interests and concerns are, and point out where you both have common interests.

- Tell the people you work with what your hopes and desires are for the work you're doing together. Ask them theirs.

- If you manage people, clearly tell them what you expect from them and what they can expect from you. Then follow through. This may sound a lot like the behavior of sincerity and reliability, and to some degree it is. Exhibiting the behaviors of reliability and sincerity are ways of demonstrating that you have their interests in mind.

- When you make decisions or take action, let people know you understand how it affects them, even if the effect is adverse. Tell them why you are doing what you're doing, and identify the interests your actions serve.

CHAPTER 3

Sincerity

I mean what I say, say what I mean, and act accordingly

Authentic leaders have a steady and confident presence. They do not show up as one person one day and another person the next.

—Bill George, Peter Sims, Andrew N. McLean, and Diana Mayer

Sincerity is the assessment you make about another person's honesty and integrity. When you trust their sincerity, you are saying you believe that what they do will align with what they say. It is also an assessment that when they speak, you can trust what they say is true to the best of their knowledge. In other words, they don't willfully misrepresent information.

Here are three examples of how clients of mine have referred to sincerity:

- "What I really appreciate about Tom is he doesn't just talk about how things need to change and expect others to go do it. He makes it happen. When he started here two years ago, he publicly declared to the entire company that he wanted this to be a place where everyone's ideas would be heard, respected, and considered. A lot of people were skeptical at first, me included. But he was sincere about it. He actually did what was needed to get us to buy in and make it happen. And it's paid off. We've gotten lots of great ideas for saving money and improving processes, even new products, from people all over the company—manufacturing folks, customer service reps, a receptionist, several middle managers."

- "One of the things that makes Elaine believable is she doesn't sugarcoat things. Her talk at the recent company-wide meeting was a breath of fresh air. She acknowledged that we are in trouble and actually named some of the specific problems. But she also gave us some good news I could believe. When she told us why she thinks we can turn things around, I found myself believing that too. I got really excited."

- "The senior VP of sales and marketing says our division is critical to the overall success of the company, but he sure doesn't act like we are. When we ask for something from corporate marketing or sales, he talks like they'll support what we're doing, but then he turns around and pulls the rug out from under us. For example, this year we proposed a new incentive plan for the sales force that would have compensated them better for selling our division's products without costing the company any more. When our GM and I talked to the VP about it, he said he would implement it. But at the last minute he revamped the comp plan and completely gutted the part that would have incentivized the sales force to sell our division's products. His excuse was that it was impractical, but at this point I don't believe he ever meant to keep it in the plan."

CONGRUENCE

The assessment of sincerity is that you are telling the truth as you see it and that you mean what you say. Giving others reason to assess that you are sincere is a matter of being internally and externally congruent. Internal congruence means being honest with yourself, checking your intentions, and making sure you believe and are committed to what you are saying. External congruence means being honest and straightforward with others. Another way to say this is that you don't have a different conversation in your head than the one you are having out loud.

When people believe you aren't sincere, everything you say becomes suspect, and your effectiveness in the workplace is drastically diminished. Intentional deceit, when discovered, immediately leads people to assess that you are not sincere and can't be believed, even if you think you are telling harmless lies to avoid upsetting people. Being found out often results in people distrusting your sincerity in all matters.

Being sincere means your words and actions are aligned. You walk your talk. It also means what you say is consistent from one person to another and consistent over time. If you change your mind, as we all do from time to time, maintaining others' trust in your sincerity requires that you let them know you are committed to something different from before. Being sincere takes intention, attention, and dedication, as does cultivating any aspect of trust in a complex, fast-paced environment with sometimes competing commitments.

ALIGNING WORDS AND ACTIONS

People will question your sincerity when you don't act in accordance with what you say. One of the most common breakdowns in trust comes when people, particularly leaders, don't walk their talk. So what's going on? Simply put, people too often fail to recognize that when they express their intentions, expectations, desires, beliefs, and values, they aren't just describing themselves; they are creating expectations about their future behavior in the minds of those who listen to them. If you fail to fulfill those expectations, people will assume you were not sincere in what you said.

If you are a leader, you need to understand that the people you lead watch you very closely and are acutely aware of how congruent your actions are with your words. The greater your span of influence and responsibility in your organization, the more people will be observing what you say and do. I believe this amount of scrutiny is one of the main reasons that the survey quoted in the introduction indicates that top leaders were considered the least trustworthy. While leaders want to be seen as sincere, when they don't take the time to fully consider how the consequences of their actions align with what they say, they expose themselves to judgments of insincerity.

For example, Ellen tells a story about being promoted into the role of new director for her agency and "learning once again," as she put it, the critical importance of aligning her words and actions. She had been deputy director to the former agency head, who had left behind more enemies than friends when he resigned under pressure from the board. The former director had been perceived as arrogant, dictatorial, and largely ignorant of the agency's fundamental mission. During his tenure he had created resentment and anger throughout the agency.

Ellen had been deputy director before her former boss had been hired, but she was closely associated with him in the minds of many in the agency. Because of this, she knew she came to the job with baggage and that she had to act quickly and decisively to gain the trust and confidence of the employees, particularly middle management. As soon as she moved into the director's office, she announced that she would do all she could to turn the agency around. She publicly asked that everyone work together to resolve and move beyond their own issues.

Ellen proceeded to make a number of positive changes in her first few months. However, she kept putting off one task. One of the agency's top managers, who had been brought in by the former director, was struggling in his position. Yet she couldn't bring herself to replace him. "I kept him on for all the wrong reasons," she said. "His wife has medical problems, so losing benefits would be difficult. They had three kids, and he was the sole income provider. And he was really trying hard. I kept trying to ignore the fact that he was in way over his head and just couldn't do the job."

Keeping him on, it turned out, was also stopping her other managers, particularly the middle managers, from completely trusting her. They saw her refusal to confront the problem as a sign that she didn't actually intend to make the necessary changes, that she was just giving lip service to fixing problems in the agency. "I'd learned that lesson earlier in my career but apparently forgot it, so I got to learn it again: people won't trust you are sincere if they don't see you walking your talk all the way."

ALIGNING WORDS WITH WORDS

Your sincerity can also be questioned if you appear to say one thing to one person and something different to another or if

---

✔ TRUST CHECK

Think about a time when someone in a leadership position in your company declared an intention, vision, value, expectation, or belief, and consider these questions:

- In your judgment, did this person take all the actions in their power to support the new direction?
- How did their words and actions affect your judgment of their sincerity?
- How did your judgment of their sincerity affect your attitude toward the company as a whole?
- How did your judgment of their sincerity affect your work?
- Have you had to learn Ellen's lesson the hard way? What will you do differently next time?

---

what you say isn't consistent over time. The key word here is *appear*. You may find that by carelessly changing what you say or how you say it—even slightly—different people may come away with conflicting ideas of what you meant. Here is an example of someone who considered himself trustworthy and had no idea the way he talked with his employees was causing them to distrust his sincerity.

Roger was director of a department within a large government agency. He had been in the position for about two years and oversaw a group of managers who ran different programs but often had to work together to meet their program goals. Roger was, by his own admission, uncomfortable with conflict and didn't like to disappoint people. He began working with a coach after a 360-degree survey revealed that his staff had little trust in him, a surprise only to Roger.

Roger was aware there was conflict and distrust within his team. They spent an inordinate amount of time engaged in negative interpersonal conflict, politicking and undermining each other's efforts. But he was floored to discover that they didn't trust him any more than they did each other. It became quickly apparent to Roger's coach, and eventually to Roger himself, that a big part of the problem was that his team did not consider him sincere. As one put it, "He won't tell you the truth half the time, and the other half of the time he won't tell you anything at all."

When the team couldn't decide on how something should be done, Roger would talk with each manager individually to "get their input." In his desire to avoid conflict and not disappoint people, Roger would talk to each one in a way that sounded as if he was making a decision that favored them. He thought he was just "collecting everyone's ideas," and he would make a final decision after he'd heard from everyone involved. However, each manager left Roger's office believing he supported their idea or approach, only to find out the other managers had a different story. The problem was usually further exacerbated because Roger would often fail to announce his final decision, leaving his staff without clear direction until they could figure out what he was doing.

Once Roger understood the distinction of sincerity, he could see how what he was saying and doing was causing his direct reports to judge him as not trustworthy. He could also see a way to repair the damage and begin to rebuild their trust in him.

BUILDING TRUST: SINCERITY

Here are some ways to build and maintain trust in terms of sincerity:

- Be intentional about what you say to people. Factual inaccuracies and omissions, when revealed, inevitably lead others to doubt your sincerity. Before you relate a fact, do what you can to make sure it is accurate. In the haste of the moment, you might be tempted to say what you think is *probably* true. But doing this often and being wrong will lead to others doubting your sincerity. Omitting relevant facts can also be tempting, especially if you think they might confuse the issue or add unnecessary work. But, again, do this even once, and people may judge you as not sincere.

- Be intentional about what you say when you talk about your interests, expectations, ideas, beliefs, and values. Before you speak, think about what expectations you may create in your listeners' minds. Ask yourself, What expectations do I want to create? How committed am I to what I'm talking about? What will I commit to do to make what I talk about a reality? If you do not want to create an expectation, preface your comments with something like "I haven't thought this through all the way, but here are some of my ideas . . ."

- Check with people regularly to align expectations with intentions. If they're not aligned, begin a conversation about the differences as soon as possible: "When I said I wanted this to be a collaborative effort, I expected that we would all share our ideas and information openly. Is that what you expected?" or "It sounds like when I said 'collaborative,' you expected we would decide everything by group consensus. This was not part of what I intended, so we should talk about that."

- Check your internal congruence, your doubt-o-meter. Ask yourself, How sure am I about what I'm saying? If you do have doubts, should you share them with the person you're speaking to? Others can easily spot any incongruence between what you say and how you say it. When you have internal doubts, your nonverbal communication gives you away far more often than you realize. Prefacing your statement with "I'm not completely sure about this, but here's what I think..." is usually better than trying to sound sure about something when you're not.

- Check your external congruence. Is what you're saying consistent with what you've said to this person or someone else in the past? If you know what you are about to say is not consistent with something you've said before, ask yourself why. Have you changed your mind? Explain the reason for your inconsistency. This may mean getting back to people to let them know you've changed your mind and why.

  Here's an example: "Yesterday I told you some management team members thought the VP had punished them for expressing their concerns about her behavior. I'd like to correct that. No one actually said they had been punished. I inferred that from what they did say. What they actually said to me was..."

- Ask people to tell you how they interpret what you say. Roger's story is a good example of someone who failed to understand how his language was interpreted in a way that was completely unintended and created distrust when he wanted to build trust. You can do this by asking them these types of questions: "When I say, 'I agree with you,' what do you think I mean?" Or, "When I told you I was really concerned about this, did you think I meant you should take some action on it right now?"

✅ TRUST CHECK

Here is a way to check whether what you think and what you say are aligned:

- We usually have some inkling when we have been less than sincere with someone, even if we know we didn't intentionally deceive them in any way. It may come as an uncomfortable body sensation or a feeling of unease during or after the conversation. Recall a time when you had this feeling.
- Take a piece of paper and draw a line down the center, top to bottom, so you have two columns. At the top of the left-hand column, write "What I Thought." At the top of the right-hand column, write "What Was Said."[1] In the right column write out what you and the other person said in your conversation as best you can recall it. Then write in the left column what you were actually thinking each time you said something. If there were times when you were thinking something but didn't say it, write your thoughts in the left-hand column and leave the right column blank at that point.
- As you look over what you said in the conversation, how congruent was it with what you were thinking? Did you have a substantially different conversation going on in your head than the one you had out loud? In all likelihood your nonverbal communication matched what was going on in your head more

accurately than what you were saying aloud, which means that the person you were talking to possibly left feeling vaguely ill at ease as well. If talking with you often leaves them feeling uneasy, they might begin to question your sincerity. You are also more likely to act in accordance with the conversation in your head, further eroding trust.

CHAPTER 4

Reliability

You can count on me to deliver what I promise

We must not promise what we ought not, lest we be called on to perform what we cannot.

—Abraham Lincoln

Reliability is the assessment that you fulfill the commitments you make, that you keep your promises.

Here are three examples of how former clients refer to reliability:

- "At the end of every team meeting, we go around and make sure everyone knows what actions to take. The great thing about the people on this team is that they almost always do what they commit to. It's really extraordinary, which is a sad thing to say because it should be ordinary."
- "One of the things I can trust about Cindy is that when she makes a commitment, you can be sure she'll follow through. And if she can't because something unexpected comes up, she'll let you know as soon as she knows."

- "I used to believe Kelly when she said she'd help me out with this or that. But after being burned a few times, I don't trust her at all anymore."

Reliability is about keeping commitments. This is not always as easy as it seems. Most people say that they keep their commitments. But ask the people who work around them, and chances are you'll find at least one or two who will tell you they don't always do such a good job. This is partly caused by a constantly changing work environment, competing commitments, and the many demands on our time and attention. People also break promises as a result of others failing to make clear requests, offers, and commitments. For example, I was observing a meeting held by a coaching client, Anne. I heard the following exchange between her and two of her directors, Larry and Cindy.

> ANNE: This is going to be a real problem for Sales.
> LARRY: Yes. We should let them know right away.
> CINDY: They're not going to like it. We'll have to be careful how we communicate it to them.
> ANNE (*looking at Larry*): You're right, they won't like it. But they need to know, and the sooner the better.
> LARRY: Yup.
> ANNE: Good. Okay, let's look at the next agenda item.

After the meeting was over, when Anne and I were back in her office, I asked her if she thought Larry had made a commitment to do something specific. She said, "Yes, he had agreed to get the message out to the sales organization today." I ventured that he may not have left the meeting with quite the same understanding. At that point Anne said, "Hmm, you're right, I don't remember specifically saying he needed to do it today." I said, "Anne, I'll bet Larry doesn't think he made any commitment about this at all," and suggested she ask him what he thought had happened. Anne said she'd bet me a lunch that Larry did understand he'd made a commitment.

We walked down the hall to Larry's office, and Anne asked him if he was clear about what she expected he'd do. Larry said he knew Anne thought the situation needed to be dealt with but didn't believe he'd made a commitment to do anything in particular. His plan was to contact a couple of salespeople and ask their advice on how best to communicate the problem. Beyond that he figured Anne would make a final decision on what to do. I enjoyed my lunch!

REQUESTS, OFFERS, AND COMMITMENTS

Interestingly, one of the things Anne wanted to work on in coaching was her concern that her team often failed to do what she told them to do. This provided an excellent opportunity to work with her on the language of requests, offers, and commitments. You make commitments in two ways: in response to someone else's request (or, if they are higher up in the organization, it might be direction or a command) or by making an offer to someone. When the other person accepts your offer, they usually consider it a commitment on your part.

Ideally when someone makes a request or gives you direction, they include all the information you need to determine whether you can commit to fulfilling it or not. If you say yes, they will assume you have committed to do exactly what they had asked of you or what they think they asked, even if they didn't say it all in their request. But here is the problem: if the request is unclear and you say yes anyway, they will still assume you have committed to do exactly what they had asked—only you won't be clear on all the specifics of what they want. Without that information, you risk failing to deliver what they think you committed to delivering. If this happens often enough, they will begin to assess you as unreliable.

The language of requests, offers, and commitments is at the heart of this assessment and requires some space and attention.

INCREASING RELIABILITY THROUGH THE CYCLE OF COMMITMENT

Unclear or incomplete requests, offers, and commitments are often the source of unintended breaches of trust. Dr. Fernando Flores, a thought leader in business process design and coaching, initially spoke about the need to make clear, complete requests, offers, and promises and introduced the idea of a *promise cycle* in his book with Terry Winograd, *Understanding Computers and Cognition*, and in various papers and lectures. Several other authors and teachers, including Robert Dunham, Julio Olalla, and Rafael Echeverria,[1] have added to ideas and developed versions of what I call the *Cycle of Commitment*. I am indebted to their work and have adapted it to show how the language of requests, offers, and promises can help you consistently make commitments that are realistic and achievable. Doing so increases your ability to fulfill them, helping you earn the trust of the people you work with. Using it also allows you to make requests that set others up to successfully accomplish them.

Requests and responses are part of an action cycle that starts the process of getting something done. The cycle begins with a customer who determines a need. They identify someone who can fulfill their request, an intended performer. People make requests to get someone else's help. The term *request*

☑ TRUST CHECK

Think of a request someone recently made of you that you had difficulty fulfilling. As you read the section below on requests, answer the questions as they relate to this request. Some answers may be obvious, but you may also find some surprises.

---

refers to a range of speech acts that includes commands, direction, and pleas, depending on the context in which they are made. Whatever the context and type, making a request starts the process of getting tasks done. If you do commit to doing what another person requests and then in their eyes fail to keep the commitment, they may lose some degree of trust in your reliability.

CLEAR AND COMPLETE REQUESTS

From years of experience, we know that some ways of making requests work well and others don't. Below are the basic elements that make for clear, complete, and direct requests that do work well.

> *Customer*—Who is asking? The identity of the customer may seem obvious, but it isn't always. For example, who is the customer when someone says, "We need to do some research on this"? You should know who the customer is, if for no other reason than to know whom you can go to if you have additional questions or concerns about the request.

Performer—Who is being asked to fulfill the request? Are you clear that you are the intended performer? Are you the right person to do this? If not, whom should the request be directed to?

Action—What does the customer want you to do? Is it something the performer has the time, ability, and resources to do?

Conditions of satisfaction—How will both the customer and performer know the task has been done to the customer's satisfaction? Unless the customer makes it absolutely clear what conditions will satisfy them, then the performer is left to fill in the specifics. With luck this will result in what is wanted, but being clear about the conditions of satisfaction will greatly increase the chances.

Time frame—By when does the customer want it completed? Without this information, again the performer is left to decide when to do it. "ASAP" is not a useful time frame unless you are clear about what that means to the customer. If not, you may find the customer upset because you thought ASAP meant by the end of the week, and the customer was expecting it by the end of the day. Or you may put other work on a back burner to get it done by the end of the day only to learn your customer was thinking the end of the week.

Context—Having context about a request can be useful: why the customer is making it in the first place. Taken out of context, many requests can seem like people are asking you to do random tasks. Explanations on how the request fits into the bigger picture of the work you, the person making the request, and others are doing go a long way.

If you have questions about any of these elements, and you don't get clarification from the customer, you are setting yourself up to make a commitment that you may not be able to fulfill to their satisfaction. And that can lead to eroded trust.

MORE EFFECTIVE REQUESTS

Since we are also customers, we can learn how to make more effective requests. Direct requests have a much better chance of being fulfilled than those that are indirect. Yet we often soften our requests because we believe that direct requests sound rude, harsh, or at best impolite.

Keep in mind that what is considered acceptably direct language varies widely from culture to culture around the world. I'm describing how to make an effectively direct request in typical western European and North American organizational cultures. However, since many companies today are multicultural and may have customers, vendors, or other partners around the world, effective request language may differ within companies, work groups, teams, or even between manager and team member. To help avoid unintended breaches of trust that result from unclear requests, you and the people you interact with should have a mutual understanding of what constitutes a request that works in your environment.[2] Here are some examples of the three different types of requests:

- *Direct requests*, which tend to work best
    - "I ask that you ..."
    - "I request ..."
    - "Will you (please) ..."
    - "(Please) do this ..."

- *Indirect requests*, which are less clear but are often used because they sound, not surprisingly, less direct
  - "I want . . ." or "I need . . ."
  - "Why don't you . . . ?"
  - ". . . needs to be done."

  Even though none of these examples are technically requests, everyone (with the possible exception of teenagers) understands the intention behind them.
- *Really indirect requests*, which are the kind others often don't even hear as requests
  - "My coffee cup is empty." (Unspoken request: "Will you get me some more coffee?")
  - "The conference room is a real mess." (Unspoken request: "Will you clean up after your meetings?")
  - "It's almost nine o'clock." (Unspoken request: "Will you get me the status report for our 9:00 a.m. staff meeting?")

When you make a request of someone, in addition to making sure you have all the elements clear in your request, check to be sure you are fully committed to what you ask for. For example, if you ask someone to do something by the next day when you don't actually need it until next week or, worse yet, you don't need it at all, that person is likely to begin to distrust your competence, your sincerity, or both.

RESPONDING TO A REQUEST

Once a customer makes a request, the next action in the Cycle of Commitment is for you, the performer, to respond. The customer is asking you to do something specific, and you need to evaluate whether you can do it. Here are the possible responses:

☑ TRUST CHECK

Every time you say yes to one request you are saying no to something else. At some point there are too many things to do, and you have to start putting some of them off. You may fulfill your boss's request and keep their trust but not perform other commitments and possibly damage trust with others in the process. With this knowledge, reflect on the following questions:

- How do people in your organization usually make requests?
- What kind of requests do you usually make?

Commit—"Yes, I'll do it." To the customer, yes is your commitment, your promise. To them it means, "I commit to do exactly what you asked me to do." If the customer made a clear, complete request, you should have all the information you need to determine whether you can make a commitment. If something is missing from the request, you have to ask for it.

Decline—"No, I can't (or won't) do it." Saying no lets the other person know you aren't available to do what they request, and they can now find someone else to ask. The difficulty here is that often in the workplace, saying no is not considered an option, especially when the customer is someone with more authority than you. But if you say yes even though you don't think you have the time, resources, or ability to do what is being asked, you set yourself up for a different problem.

Counteroffer—"I can't do that, but I can do [alternative] instead." When a direct no isn't a viable option, and you can't commit to what the customer is asking without setting yourself up for failure, you can make a counteroffer. A counteroffer is an opportunity to create something that you believe will work. For example, you might say, "Given all the other tasks I have on my plate this week, I can't get the next quarter revenue projections to you by Friday. Will Monday morning work?" If the request is from your boss, you could say, "Given all the other tasks I have on my plate this week, I can't get the next quarter revenue projections to you by Friday unless you're willing to let my project report wait until next week." Once you make a counteroffer, it opens negotiations between you and the customer, which should ultimately result in a commitment (yes) or a decline (no).

Commit to commit—"I need to check on something before I can commit. I will let you know by [specific time]." You may need more information before you can commit to someone's request. This is where you let them know and commit to get back to them.

A trap people fall into often at work is making what I call *heroic commitments*—ones that will take heroic efforts to fulfill. You might be tempted to make heroic commitments for many reasons: you're understaffed, the customer wants it yesterday, the person asking is your boss's boss. The problem is heroic commitments set you up to either (1) fail to deliver, (2) break other commitments to get this one done, or (3) exhaust yourself to deliver on everything. I hope you're seeing the irony here. All these choices contribute to making your situation worse. While people most often choose number three, doing this regularly leads to burnout, illness, or both, which means even fewer people available to get everything done.

THE DRIVE-BY REQUEST

Novelist and newspaper editor Edgar Watson Howe reportedly once said, "Half the promises people say were never kept were never made." A request should be set up for a response. All too often at work, however, people make what I call *drive-by requests*. For example, consider the following email to Dan from his boss, read at 1:55 p.m. Pacific time, just before Dan has to go into an important meeting the boss asked him to cover for her. "Dan, please call Lynn in the New York office and find out what's going on with the Wizbie account. Then could you draft a one-pager on it and email it to me? I need it for my meeting with the COO at 4 p.m. Thanks."

Dan's boss hasn't given him an opportunity to respond at all. A yes response is just assumed. In this case the request is a setup for frustration and possible failure. Does this sound familiar? It could just as well be a voicemail, text message, or even the boss sticking her head into Dan's office, making the request, and disappearing before Dan can respond. What can he do? He can choose to miss the first part of the meeting to call Lynn right away. Hopefully he'll be able to reach her since it's almost 5 p.m. in New York. He'll arrive late for the meeting and possibly chalk up some distrust points with some of the other attendees.

That was the choice Dan made. He called Lynn to get the information his boss asked for and then went to the meeting, where he planned to discreetly write the email memo to his boss on his laptop. When he arrived in the conference room, almost twenty minutes late, everyone had been waiting for him because the main item for discussion required his input. One of the people in the meeting made a sarcastic comment about Dan's tardiness. In the end Dan didn't have any time to write the email to his boss. When the meeting finally ended, he dashed off the email, getting it to his boss just minutes before her four o'clock meeting.

The next day his boss asked Dan to see her first thing. When he got to her office, she was visibly angry. She told him she got the email about the Wizbie account so late she didn't have time to use it to prepare for her meeting with the COO. She ended her brief tirade by saying, "I expect more responsiveness from you." Dan didn't know what to say. He left her office angry, confused, and very close to quitting his job.

After cooling down, Dan recalled what he knew about the Cycle of Commitment to recognize what had happened and how to fix it. The next day he asked his boss if he could talk with her about the situation. He described his dilemma and the stress and frustration it had created. He talked about how giving him a chance to respond to her request rather than assuming a yes could have saved them both some heartburn because he could have let her know about the conflict and asked for her direction. To his relief, Dan's boss acknowledged the problem and apologized. More importantly, she realized the importance of waiting for responses to requests.

Ultimately, like Dan, you can choose to live with the stress, or you can have a conversation with the people who make drive-by requests and ask that when they give you a task, they wait for your response rather than just assuming a yes.

REVOKING AND RENEGOTIATING

How often has someone made a commitment to you and then told you when it was due that they hadn't been able to do it?

☑ TRUST CHECK

Take a moment to reflect on drive-by requests at your workplace:

- Have drive-by requests like this created inordinate stress and frustration for you?
- How often have you failed to fulfill requests that came to you this way?
- What has it done to others' assessment of your trustworthiness?
- Has it affected your trust in those people?
- If people do send you drive-by requests, what do you do?
- How often do you make drive-by requests of others?

How has that affected your level of trust in them? When you make a commitment and set to work on it, you may encounter a problem that is out of your control that will prevent you from fulfilling the commitment. In that case you need to renegotiate or revoke your commitment. Revoking or renegotiating a commitment should be done as soon as you realize you will not be able to fulfill it.

Revoking or renegotiating while the customer still has other options for getting what they want maintains their trust. If you wait too long to let the customer know about the problem, you'll reach a point where they cannot get what they need done by their deadline from you or anyone else. At this point there is no possibility of renegotiating the commitment; you can only revoke it. However, even revoking after this point will usually maintain some degree of trust if you do so before the final due date. But when you fail to revoke or renegotiate at all, you may leave your customer in a difficult situation. Most people will be forgiving once or twice. But eventually they will begin to lose trust in the reliability of your commitments.

People often find that revoking their commitment is difficult to do even when they know that the circumstances preventing them from delivering on time are not within their control. Some people fear being seen as someone who can't deliver. Others have an unrealistic idea of what they are truly capable of getting done. And some simply hate to disappoint others. Ironically, these ways of thinking are often the same ones that lead people to make unrealistic commitments in the first place.

No matter the reason they don't want to revoke their commitment, the problem is they go forward as if somehow something magical will happen to solve the problem. "Maybe she will call in sick today, and I'll have another day to work on it" they'll tell themselves. Or "Maybe if I work really hard in the next hour and don't get interrupted by anyone, I can still get this work done."

What I've found works best is when an organization's leaders make it clear that they would prefer everyone to acknowledge when they honestly can't meet their commitments, and people who revoke commitments will not be punished. If someone has to revoke commitments often, it can be an indication they need help. It may be that they are afraid they'll be seen as someone who can't deliver, they are chronically unrealistic about what they can do, or something in the organization's systems or culture is getting in their way. This can be a good opportunity to address the problem and correct it.

REPORTING COMPLETION AND CHECKING SATISFACTION

Two more practices that will build and maintain trust with your customers in the Cycle of Commitment are reporting to them when you've completed your commitment and checking for their satisfaction. Some commitments involve delivering the product directly to your customer. Other times, you commit to deliver your product to someone else. In the latter case, if you make a practice of telling your customers when you've delivered on your commitment, it builds your trustworthiness. Checking that your customer is satisfied with what you've done also tends to build trust by letting them know you are committed to their satisfaction.

BUILDING TRUST: RELIABILITY

Here are some ways to build and maintain trust in terms of reliability, even in the face of constantly changing priorities and opposing demands:

- Before you respond to a request, make sure you can do what is asked. Ask yourself, Do I have the time and resources to do this? Can I meet the requested deadline? If not, negotiate something you can do. You might also ask yourself, Is it important to agree to this request no matter what else is on my plate? If so, what can I renegotiate with someone else so I can do this?
- If someone makes a request of you that isn't clear, ask for clarification: "I'd just like to verify, when do you want the report? Are you expecting one page with bullet points on

each project's status or an in-depth report on each project? Do you want me to email copies to all the attendees before the meeting or just send it to you?"

- When you make offers to other people, be clear about what it is you will do and possibly what you won't do as well. Remember, when they accept your offer, it will become a commitment in their minds.
- Listen and determine what kind of conversations the people you are talking to think they are having. Are they talking about a problem and why it occurred? Are they talking about possibilities for the future? Or are they making requests or offers and trying to nail down commitments? How do you need to respond?

CHAPTER 5

Competence

I know I can do this—I don't know if I can do that

Often the desire to appear competent impedes our ability to become competent, because we are more anxious to display our knowledge than to learn what we do not know.

—Magdeleine Sable

When you trust someone is competent, it means you believe they have the ability to do a particular task or job. Trust in a person's competence usually also means you expect they will tell you if they can't do something and ask for help.

Here are three examples of how three people I know have referred to competence:

- "I brought Linda in to run the office after Ron left so suddenly because I trust her ability as a leader to get the best out of people even in the most difficult situations. I know she'll come through for them and for us."

- "I'm putting Raj on this project because I trust that if anyone can fix this mess, he can. He is my most competent engineering manager. What I ask is that you trust his lead and do what he asks."
- "Paul may have been a competent salesperson, but he certainly wasn't a competent district manager, so I don't know how he got promoted to regional VP. The only thing I can imagine is the senior VP of sales doesn't know how incompetent he is, which makes me wonder how competent our senior VP is."

Being judged as competent means doing what you do well enough to satisfy the standards of the person who is judging you. Someone assesses you as competent when you have the skills, knowledge, and abilities to act effectively within a specific domain, such as accounting, marketing, project management, or leading people.

People judge us as competent in one domain but not in others. However, sometimes this tendency can cause people to confer an assessment of competence on you in an area where you don't claim competence. For example, a highly skilled engineer is promoted to a management position because people assume his competence in engineering means he will be good at managing engineers. Managing others is a different skill set from engineering. If this has happened to you, the best thing you can do is be clear about what you know you can do and what you have yet to learn.

Being competent does not mean being perfect. Part of doing something well is knowing what you don't know, being willing to learn, and asking for help when you need it. For example, Luisa was a highly competent engineer who had been promoted in two rapid steps, first to group manager and then fifteen months later to director of development engineering. She had seven direct reports and oversaw a team of twenty-eight engineers. Luisa knew her competence as a development engineer still granted her some credibility with the engineers who worked for her.

She also realized that at the director level she was being judged on her competency as a manager and leader of people. And she knew she was still not sufficiently competent as a leader to be a strong director.

But one of Luisa's great strengths was her ability to admit to herself and others what she didn't know. She was open to learning and asked for help, feedback, direction, and suggestions from her manager and employees. Luisa sought mentoring from others, took courses, and read books. When she had exhausted those sources for learning, she convinced her manager to approve funding for her to work with a leadership coach.

By publicly acknowledging her initial lack of competence as a leader at the director level, asking for help when she needed

---

✅ TRUST CHECK

Think about someone you've worked with or for who you thought wasn't competent to do their job, and consider the following questions:

- What were the standards you used to assess their competence?
- Where did those standards come from?
- Were they appropriate standards to use in this case?
- Did the other person understand and accept these standards?

it, and taking steps to develop this competence, Luisa built and maintained the trust of her manager, peers, and the people who worked for her. As she developed into a competent leader, her career continued to advance.

BUILDING TRUST: COMPETENCE

Here is what you can do to help build trust in your competence:

- Make a list to clarify to yourself and others the areas you claim competence in.
- Define the standards by which your competence is assessed. That may mean comparing your standards with others. When standards are clear and agreed on by everyone concerned, an assessment of competence or incompetence is easy to make. On the other hand, when standards for the task, job, or role being performed are unclear, or people disagree about them, it can easily lead to having at least some people distrusting your competence.
- When you don't know something, say so and ask for help, clarification, training, or whatever you need to perform what was asked. Cultivating trust in your competence doesn't mean you have to be fully competent from the get-go. It does require being honest with others about what you can and can't do and what you know and don't know.
- Ask for feedback from others about your performance. Don't wait for them to tell you that you are making mistakes. Often people won't tell you your performance isn't good enough until you've made some big mistakes, and they actively distrust your competence.

CHAPTER 6

Confronting Distrust

Mistrust doubles the cost of doing business.

—John O. Whitney

D istrust is a choice to not make yourself vulnerable to another person's actions. It is the general assessment that something you value is not safe with this person in this situation or any other situation. When we distrust, we engage in strategies to protect ourselves, which inevitably impede everyone's ability to get good work done. This is part of the cost of distrust in the workplace.

THE COST OF DISTRUST

Tony Simons, the Lewis G. Schaeneman Jr. Professor of Innovation and Dynamic Management at Cornell University's School of Hotel Administration, researched the effect of trust on a company's bottom line. One study Simons did found that of seventy-six hotels surveyed, those where employees strongly believed their managers followed through on promises (reliability) and demonstrated the values they preached (sincerity) were substantially more profitable than those whose managers were less reliable or sincere. Even a very small improvement in a hotel's score on

Simons's scale could be expected to increase its bottom-line profit significantly.

Simons used the term *behavioral integrity* to describe a particular set of behaviors I have called *reliability* (keeping promises) and *sincerity* (being honest and acting with integrity by demonstrating espoused values). He noted, "Employee perceptions of their managers' integrity—both keeping promises and demonstrating espoused values—were strongly linked to hotel profitability. Employees' belief in managers' integrity, and their trust in managers, have a lot more impact on profits than more traditional issues like employee 'satisfaction' or even 'commitment.'"[1] In those organizations where employees believe their managers to be trustworthy, everyone was a beneficiary.

As Simons's studies and other research on employee engagement show, maintaining high trust at work creates a direct value.[2] People who are deeply engaged in their work feel committed to and positive about what they are doing and those they are doing it with. They also tend to derive a positive sense of purpose from their work. Yet people fail to have intentional conversations to build and maintain trust even when they believe trust is low. Instead they pretend outwardly that trust exists even though they know it doesn't. Robert Solomon and Fernando Flores, authors of the book *Building Trust*, called this *cordial hypocrisy*.[3]

Distrust and fear go hand in hand. Whenever distrust of any kind creeps into relationships in the workplace, it produces attitudes and behaviors guaranteed to undermine effective work, including suspicion, resistance, defensiveness, interpersonal conflict, withholding of information, and overzealous checking of others' work. When distrust becomes part of an organization's culture, it leads to increasingly elaborate and draconian control mechanisms. People's time, energy, and creativity are channeled

☑ TRUST CHECK

Think of a person you do not trust, and consider the following questions:

- Is it blanket distrust, or can you identify one of your specific values or tasks that you don't trust them with?
- Specifically, what do you value that you do not trust them with?
- What are you concerned they might do with what you value?
- What does this person say or do that causes you to distrust them?
- What do you do to avoid being harmed by this person's actions?

into actions that may make them feel somewhat safer but do not produce what they truly want and need—good working relationships based on trust.

Most people will agree that working with someone we distrust is an unpleasant experience. Yet so often we avoid actually talking with that individual about our concerns. How often have you had a direct conversation with someone you don't trust? If you're like most people, you rarely do. This has a great deal to do with how we think about distrust and the language we have for talking about it. I asked several people what they mean when they say they don't trust someone. Here are some of their responses:

✅ TRUST CHECK

Consider what it means when you say you don't trust a particular person.

- If you were to have a conversation about trust with someone you distrust, what would you want to say?
- If someone you work with were to tell you they didn't trust you, how would you respond?
- What would you ask them so you could understand their specific concern about your words or actions?
- What could be the benefit of doing this?
- What could it cost you?

- "He cheats."
- "She is sneaky and mean."
- "He is a liar."
- "She only cares about herself."
- "I can't believe anything she says."
- "He just doesn't do anything right."

Given this, it isn't surprising people seldom talk directly about distrust. If it requires you to tell someone you don't trust them, and you imagine the other person defines untrustworthiness in the same way (which they probably do), you're probably going to think twice about it. What people often tell me is "It would hurt his feelings," "That's too mean to say to someone," or simply "I can't just go tell her that." Telling someone you don't trust them can feel uncomfortable and vulnerable. Given the choice, many people would rather have a root canal. We assume such a conversation will lead to outright conflict or withdrawal and make the situation worse.

Using the distinctions of care, sincerity, reliability, and competence can make talking about distrust less risky and much more constructive. With clear examples of the behaviors your distrust is based on, you can talk with the person in a way that they are more likely to hear. This, in turn, can create a path to building or rebuilding trust. As one manager, George, described it, "At first, I ignored my sense that I didn't trust this guy, but I kept finding more evidence that I couldn't trust him. Then I tried not interacting with him. I guess I hoped that somehow he'd figure out he wasn't trusted and change. But that worked only for a few weeks because my team needed his help to get our work done. I went to my boss about it, but he told me to work it out."

George's frustration almost led him to quit before he tried actually talking to the person he distrusted. "At one point I got into a yelling match with him about something completely unrelated to what I needed him to do. That night I went home and told my wife I was going to start looking for another job. But about that time, coincidentally, I started working with a coach, and the first thing we worked on was talking with this guy about trust. I really didn't want to, and I almost felt physically sick before I met with him, but in the end it worked." What made the difference for George was to first understand specifically what he distrusted in his coworker—care, sincerity, reliability, or competence—and then articulate it in a way that didn't provoke the person into defensiveness. Knowing these distinctions can be enormously valuable when you want to talk constructively about issues of trust with others.

It is also important to distinguish whether you believe the other person's actions resulted in an unintended breach of your trust or a deliberate betrayal. In today's workplace, acting in a way that breaches trust without intending it can easily happen. This is different from a conscious act of betrayal. Determining which you believe happened will have a big impact on the conversation you have.

HOW YOU SAY IT COUNTS

Consider the following example of someone talking about distrust. A team leader who was trying to work through trust issues with a member of her team before she had learned the four assessments of trust made the statement, "Based on what we've seen lately, I don't think we can really trust you to get anything done. Maybe you aren't putting this team high enough on your priority list."

After some coaching, the team leader revised her statement and tried again: "Based on two recent situations where you didn't deliver what we thought you'd committed to, I am concerned that we can't rely on you to keep the commitments you make to this team. But I would like to hear your perspective on this."

Which of these statements would be less likely to make you defensive? Which would give you more useful information? Which would be more likely to lead to a productive conversation about the trust concerns the speaker has? The two statements are not wildly different, but the second one offers the listener a more specific assessment that points directly to a category of behavior: reliability. By taking the discussion from under the umbrella of trust and distinguishing it as a specific behavior, this team leader was able to initiate a constructive conversation about her real concern. By including facts that support her assessment, the team member was able to understand specifically what the concern was and respond directly to it. Below are two checklists to help you prepare for and have a conversation about distrust.

Seven Steps to Take before the Conversation

Before talking with someone about a trust issue you have with them, here are seven steps you can take to help you prepare for the conversation:

1. Identify the assessment(s) you are concerned with:
   - Care
   - Sincerity
   - Reliability
   - Competence
2. Define the standard you are using. The point of this step is to realize that the other person may well have different standards from you. If this turns out to be the case, then you can focus your conversation to arrive at a shared understanding.
3. Identify the specific actions or behaviors that have led to your assessment of distrust. This is a critical step. Telling the person specifically what they do or say (or don't do or say) that you interpret as untrustworthy can help them understand how to rebuild trust with you.
4. Consider what you are doing that may be contributing to the situation. If you are sincerely dedicated to repairing trust and maintaining it going forward, you must take this step.
5. Determine what you need from them in order for them to regain your trust. What can they do that will address your concerns and reassure you that you can begin or resume trusting them? Think it through from the other person's perspective. Is this something they have the capacity to do? Can they do it in the context of their work environment? How can you help them regain your trust?

6. Decide if you are willing to talk to the person about it by asking yourself the following questions:
    - What might I lose by having the conversation?
    - What will I lose by continuing to distrust this person?
    - How will it benefit me, my team, and my company to work this out so I can trust this person?
7. Ask the other person if they would be willing to have a conversation with you about something that concerns you. Agree on a time and place that is mutually convenient and private. Avoid blindsiding them by bringing this up as part of a conversation about something else. You want the other person to be calm, thoughtful, and open to listening to your concern and not defensive.

Five Steps to the Conversation

Once you have taken the steps to prepare for your conversation and decided to go forward, take the following actions to help ensure it goes as well as possible:

1. Start the conversation by expressing your desire to fully trust the other person. For example, you could say, "I believe in order for us to get good work done here, we need to trust each other."[4]
2. Describe the specific actions or behaviors that have impacted your trust in this person using neutral language. Tell them that as a result you do not fully trust their care, sincerity, reliability, or competence at this time. For example, say, "The last three times you took on assignments for the team, you didn't get them done in the time you committed to. All three were at least a week late. Because of this, at this point I don't trust you will

meet your commitments in the future." Talk about what they have done, not who they are.

3. Ask them to tell you how they see the situation you described. Their response to this may be an attempt to excuse their behavior or blame other people, their circumstances, or possibly even you. *No matter what they say at this point, listen without interrupting, contradicting, or defending yourself until they have finished.* Consider what they have said and respond honestly. You can also acknowledge what you identified earlier as the ways you recognize you may be contributing to the trust breakdown. This is usually just the beginning of what can be a productive series of conversations. Remember, the conversation is about building trust, not about confirming that you are right.

   What do you do if you've listened to the other person, and they have not taken any responsibility for their behavior, but instead only offered excuses or blamed others? If the relationship is important enough to you or your work, you will need to risk some conflict. Repeat that there is an issue of trust in the relationship between the two of you that needs to be dealt with somehow because it is getting in the way of you both doing your best work. Ask if there is anything they could do in the situation to address your concerns. If you believe you can do so, offer to help determine what is not in their control and address it.

4. Describe what they can do to regain your trust. For example, you could say, "To help me fully trust your (care, reliability, competence, or sincerity), here is what you can do . . ."

5. Ask them if they will commit to do what is needed to regain your trust.

CONVERSATION EXAMPLES

The following are examples of how to start a conversation about repairing distrust for each of the four trust distinctions. Since each distinction is slightly different, I've provided a script that lays out the five steps of the conversation using the appropriate language for each assessment. Of course, real conversations rarely stay on script, and these examples are no exception. The point is if (1) you've done the seven steps to take before the conversation, (2) you know where the script is going, and (3) you can stay open to listening to what the other person has to say, you will usually be able to get to a constructive resolution.

Care: Conversation Example

In the following example, Joan is a senior director of sales support. She reports to Art, her boss, who is a VP of sales.

> JOAN: Art, in order to get good work done here we need to trust each other. When you asked me to redefine our customer support strategy, you said it was critically important, and I needed to get a draft plan to you by March 15.
>
> My group has put in a lot of time working on this. I've submitted two interim drafts to you, which you haven't responded to at all. Then last week I heard that you and Jan and two other VPs are working on a new overall sales strategy. From what I've heard, Jan wants to take customer support out of sales and put it under her. None of us think that's a good idea. But since I haven't heard anything about this from you, I'm beginning to question whether you support that view when you talk with Jan. Can you tell me what's going on?

ART: Joan, I agree with you that moving customer support into Jan's group is not the best plan. I should have told you about the task force Mike assigned me to sooner. But it's a good thing he put me on it because otherwise there wouldn't be anyone to balance Jan's influence. I do still need a support strategy from you, so please complete what you're doing. In the meantime let me fight the Jan battle.

JOAN: I'm glad to hear you still back us staying in sales. In the future, it would help me maintain my trust that you have my team's interests at heart if you tell me what's going on before I hear stories about it from others.

In this conversation Joan presents her concern about Art's support. Essentially what she is saying is that she is beginning to distrust whether he cares about her interests and the interests of their group in what appears to be a high-level power struggle. It gives Art an opportunity to reassure her. If she hadn't brought it up, she might have begun to pull back from Art and lose interest in developing a new strategy for her group.

Sincerity: Conversation Example

In this example, José is an individual contributor who reports to Dale, a group director.

JOSÉ: Dale, in order to get good work done here, we need to trust each other. When you told me you intended to offer me Rita's old position, I thought you were completely sincere about it. But I heard from someone else you're planning to give it to Dennis. At first, I thought they might be wrong, but now I'm not so sure. Whom you give the position to is your decision, and I respect that. What I'm concerned about is whether I can believe what you tell me.

DALE: Whom did you hear that from?

JOSÉ: I'd rather not say who. What I will say is that it was someone I trust who said they heard it from you.

DALE: Well, whomever it was shouldn't be passing on confidential conversations to you.

JOSÉ: Whether they should have or not, Dale, the fact is that person did tell me. So rather than harboring my distrust and getting upset about what I don't know, I thought it would be better to talk with you about it.

DALE: Okay. You're right. Two months ago I did tell you I would give you Rita's position when she retired. And I shouldn't have because it was probably premature. Some things have changed since then, and at this point I haven't decided what I want to do with her position. I wasn't lying to you, but it was far too premature to make that promise. I apologize for misleading you and for not getting back to you and telling you things may have changed. At this point I ask that you trust that what I ultimately decide is what I think will be the best for the whole department.

JOSÉ: Thank you, apology accepted. In the future, if you've told me one thing but you know things are changing, please let me know sooner. In fact, the more you share with me, the more I can trust your sincerity.

At first Dale tries to deflect the problem and blame someone else. But José is clear about his concern: he wants to be able to trust Dale's sincerity. Once Dale understands his concern, he is able to apologize and ask that José trusts his care as well as his sincerity.

Reliability: Conversation Example

In this example conversation, Bill is a product manager who is leading a product development team, and Alan is the manufacturing representative to the team.

> BILL: Alan, in order to get good work done here, we need to trust each other. At this point I'm concerned about being able to rely on your commitments. In the meeting three weeks ago, you specifically committed to getting a final manufacturing cost to the team by today so we could put it together with the other cost data. Now you're telling me you won't have it until next week. This is a real problem. You know we planned to make a go/no-go decision in today's meeting, and we need that information.
>
> This isn't the first time you've been late on something and not given any advance warning, but this one's going to cause the biggest headache. We'll have to move the meeting and postpone the decision for a week. At this point I'm concerned that we can't trust your reliability. I can't be sure you'll get it to us next week either. What's going on, Alan? [Note: To help prevent a defensive reaction from Alan, this last question has to be asked in a tone of curiosity, not blame.]
>
> ALAN: I didn't know it wasn't ready until today. Ginny, the woman I hired last month to do cost analyses, messed up and didn't get started on it until yesterday.

BILL: Alan, you were the one who made the commitment to us, not Ginny. My expectation is that you manage your people so that you can meet the commitments you make. I need to be able to trust your reliability, which means keeping your commitments or, if there is some good reason why you can't keep a commitment, I expect you to let me know as soon as you know you have a problem. That means you will have to hold your people to the same standard about commitments. I can help you with that if you want.

In this conversation, Bill has the opportunity to share with Alan his concern about reliability and to tell him what he can do to maintain Bill's trust: meet his commitments in the future or let Bill know he's run into a problem before the deliverable is due. He also makes it clear that he considers it Alan's responsibility to manage the commitments his people make to him and offers to help Alan with this.

Competence: Conversation Example

In this example conversation, Keisha is director of an IT team that is responsible for her company's internal and external websites, and Connie is a new engineer who reports to her.

KEISHA: Connie, in order to get good work done, here we need to really trust each other. Two weeks ago, I asked you to redesign and write new code for the interface for our company intranet. I asked if you thought you could get it done by the tenth, and you said you could. On the tenth, you told me you thought you'd need another week. And now you're asking for two more days. Yesterday Bob

told me he's spent four to five hours of his time helping you so far. And I know you've spent quite a few late
nights here working on it. At this point, I am concerned I
may have assigned you to a project you didn't have suffi-
cient programming skills to take on yet.

CONNIE: I admit I've had to learn a lot to do this. But I
didn't want to ask you for help. I wanted to figure it out
by myself, and I guess I also didn't want to disappoint
you.

KEISHA: I'm glad you've learned so much. But the trouble is
you didn't do it all by yourself; you used a lot of Bob's
time too. Bob is always willing to help out, but using so
much of his time is not good for the department. Plus,
the project is overdue at this point. As your manager, I
need you to tell me when you're in over your head and
need help. We can talk about it and figure out the best
way to get you what you need, but I can do it only if you
tell me.

Here Keisha is taking responsibility for giving Connie work
that was beyond her skill level and not checking in with her
sooner about it. By getting Connie's perspective, Keisha knows
she can help her understand that she wants her to ask for help.

TALKING ABOUT TRUST WITH A HIGHER-UP

Once you understand how to use the trust distinctions, you can
consider how to address trust issues with a direct report, a fellow team member, or even a peer in your company. But telling a
direct supervisor or other senior manager you don't trust them
feels like a different matter altogether. As one client put it to me,
"That would definitely be a career-limiting move."

Yet distrusting your boss is almost always a greater source of misery, depression, absenteeism, decreased performance, and attrition than distrusting anyone else in the company. And, as we've seen, it has a direct negative impact on a company's bottom line. The fear is that if you confront your boss about actions or behaviors that you find distrustful, and they react badly, you could find yourself packing up your office in no time. I don't want to trivialize that concern; it is a healthy one to have. Bosses seldom like to hear from their subordinates that they are behaving badly, and some, rather than addressing it, would prefer to fire the messenger.

But you can take some steps to decrease the risk and increase the potential benefit of talking about distrust with your boss or another person senior to you. Starting with the steps already outlined, you may want to add one or more of the following:

- Spend more time practicing. Actually write out what you might say, and check for neutral language. Describe specifically what the manager does and how it impacts your ability to get good work done. For example, you could say, "In the past week, I've scheduled a meeting with you three different times to discuss my budget. Each time, I waited in your office for at least twenty minutes. I am becoming concerned I can't rely on your commitments. I'm also concerned that I can't look for the help I need with this budget process from you. I know you are busy. So am I. How do you see this? Is there a way we can make this work better for you and for me?"
- Stay with the trust issue until you get some resolution. You might be tempted to start talking about the content issues you need to cover—for example, the budget—and leave the trust relationship conversation unresolved. If you do, it will almost inevitably surface again.

- Check in with other people who work for this same person, and find out if any of them have the same concerns you do. If so, ask if they would be willing to let you quote them or at least note that they have the same concern when you talk to the manager. If the manager is willing to meet with all of you at once, that could be even better, as long as you can all use the trust distinctions and cite specific examples. Remember, the conversation should be about what they do, not who they are.

- Ask for help and support from other senior managers or your company's human resources department. Explain to them your concerns, describing actions and specific examples using the trust distinctions.

A colleague shared with me the story of a group of mid-level managers she worked with who were often called into their division's executive leadership team to make reports, offer information, or assist the leadership team in some other way. The managers had been under a great deal of pressure from the executives to increase their efficiency and productivity and had done everything under their control to do so. But when they were called into the leadership team meetings, they often found their time was wasted waiting for executives who arrived late or came and went, they had to repeat themselves because some of the executives were multitasking and not paying attention, or they sat through entire meetings only to be told the team wasn't going to get to their part of the agenda.

Finally, after grumbling to each other about the situation for several months, one of the managers spoke to the executives on the leadership team about the problem, pointing out their behavior and letting them know one of the impacts was that all the middle managers were losing trust in their sincerity and reliability as leaders. He also asked that they change this behavior to restore trust. Doing so felt like a big risk to that manager, but the result was an apology from the higher-ups and, more important, a change in behavior on the part of the executives. The change wasn't immediate; it took a few of the executives some time to change their habitual ways of running their meetings. But with a combination of expressions of gratitude from the managers and noticeably better results from the meetings, they all came around.

Whatever conversations you have with someone whose behavior has led to your distrust, ultimately you will need to find a way to forgive them for the breach or betrayal of your trust. Forgiveness means withdrawing your attention from the past and focusing on what you are doing with them at the moment and in the future. Bernard Meltzer, the famous American radio show host, is often quoted as saying, "When you forgive, you in no way change the past—but you sure do change the future."

CHAPTER 7

When You've Betrayed Another's Trust

Calgary Health Region's patient-safety office policy requires staff to apologize to patients who have been hurt by the hospital—whether or not anyone was to blame—and to explain how it plans to avoid similar problems in the future.

—Tom Blackwell

I t is often said that it takes a long time to build trust, and it can be lost in an instant. In my experience, however, people who are intentional and rigorous in using the language of trust and who follow what they say with consistent actions build trusting relationships that endure, even in the face of betrayal. Equally important, however, is that they use another form of the language of trust when they do betray someone's trust: acknowledge and apologize. This is the flip side of the conversation you have with people you don't trust, the one you initiate with someone whose trust you feel you have damaged in some way.

The only known antidote for betrayal of someone's trust is to acknowledge it and apologize for it. To acknowledge the betrayal means recognizing what you did was wrong or damaging in the other person's eyes. Even if you didn't intend to harm them in some way, you did, and they want to know you realize this and take it seriously. To apologize is to take responsibility for what you've done, ask forgiveness, and declare your intention to redeem yourself. This, in turn, opens the possibility of a conversation about how you can make amends. Redeeming yourself in the eyes of someone you have betrayed usually means making a commitment to not repeat the action that led to betrayal. It may also entail helping fix whatever problem your actions created.

Acknowledging and apologizing are essential to restoring lost trust. When people like Randy, whom we met in chapter 1, realize they have made mistakes or acted in ways that damaged trust, they acknowledge responsibility for their actions and apologize for whatever damage it caused. Using these elements of the language of trust, they also initiate the conversation to reestablish it.

HOW TO ACKNOWLEDGE AND APOLOGIZE

Here are a few examples of how to make a clear acknowledgment and apology without excuses or justification:

- "I know I missed three meetings I scheduled with you and didn't tell you beforehand I had to cancel them. I understand this has caused you to question my sincerity and reliability. You may even be wondering if I care about your success here. I realize this has damaged our working relationship."
- "I apologize for missing those meetings and not giving you any notice. In the future, I will keep appointments I make with you if it is at all possible. If I absolutely can't make an appointment for some reason that is out of my control, I

will let you know as soon as I know. Is there anything else I can do at this point to regain your trust in these areas?"

- "I recognize I am not doing this job as well as I said I could and that you may have lost trust in my competence as a result. I did not accurately assess the scope or complexity of the work before committing to you that I could do it. I take responsibility for this and apologize for the damage it has caused. At this point I acknowledge I need help so I can continue to do this job. Specifically, I need some additional training, and I need some additional administrative assistance."

As I mentioned earlier, you may have breached another's trust in you without intending to. Even though you didn't consciously betray them and their trust, your actions will have damaged the relationship. Let the other person know you didn't mean to lose their trust by acknowledging what you did without excuses or justifications. Acknowledge the action and damage to the relationship first. Here are two examples of how to do this:

- "I realize I told you I believe in collaborative decision-making but then brought Robert into the team without consulting any of you, and in doing so I betrayed your trust in my sincerity. I understand the damage this lost trust is causing to the team and apologize. Only one team member was available, and I didn't want to put Robert on hold, so I decided to make the decision without waiting for input from you. In the future I will consult with you and consider your thoughts before bringing new people onto the team or making any other decisions that will affect the team's structure and process."

- Additionally, you could ask, "How would you like me to handle similar situations if they come up in the future?"

Making the effort to acknowledge and apologize is the first step to restoring trust. However, I want to make two notes of warning based on my experience as a coach. First, admitting we have done something to break trust with another person, even if it was unintentional, is often a humbling experience. Sometimes we find it easier to blame the other person. We might say to ourselves, "He shouldn't be so sensitive" or "She should see it wasn't my fault" or "He hasn't been honest with me either." With such thoughts, we absolve ourselves of any need to acknowledge that our actions have caused the other person to distrust us. But this only perpetuates a spiral of increasing distrust and breakdowns in communication.

Second, as I noted in the previous chapter, people are often hesitant to talk about broken trust. Sometimes the only way to recognize that you have done something that has damaged another's trust is that they act differently. The person may be less communicative, more resistant, or less cooperative than usual. At the same time, they may seem quite pleasant toward you (recall Solomon and Flores's term *cordial hypocrisy*). In this case you may have to invest some effort to get this person to admit their distrust before you can acknowledge and apologize.

CHAPTER 8

Trust, Distrust, and the Brain

The neuromanagement challenge is to design a work environment in which oxytocin can be released many times during the day.

Kenneth Nowack and Paul Zak

I've covered how to build, maintain, and restore trust by being intentional about what you say and do. Having a basic understanding of the neurobiological underpinnings of trust can often serve to increase our ability to be conscious of and make intentional choices. In this chapter, I will cover a few big takeaways from some of the neuroscience research into trust and distrust from over the last two decades.

What we experience as trust and distrust originates in our brains and nervous systems, our neurobiology, which operates in particular ways that give rise to sensations, thoughts, and feelings. Our neurobiology heavily influences our decision to trust or distrust someone. And once we have made a choice, our neurobiology will also dictate to some degree how we react to the other person. But to the extent we are aware of what's going on in our brain and nervous system, as well as that of the other person, we can increase our ability to consciously choose our responses and actions, including whether, when, and how much we are willing to trust others.

Based on a growing body of neuroscience research on trust, our brains and bodies have two parallel networks at work.[1] We have a trust network that engenders feelings of safety, openness, and a desire to connect and create together with others. The other is a distrust network, which is designed to keep us physically, emotionally, and psychologically safe by generating emotions of suspicion or fear to let us know we should be wary and defensive. Each network is identified with distinct parts of the brain, employs different neuroactive hormones, and uses different neurological pathways.[2]

Research has shown a strong correlation between trust in social interactions and the level of oxytocin in the brain. Oxytocin is a hormone and neurotransmitter found in all mammals. Oxytocin is associated with human attachment and bonding, social recognition, and trust.[3] One of the ways oxytocin works is by modulating stress hormones in the brain, specifically cortisol, making the experience of trusting another person less threatening.

The assessment of trust and its associated thoughts and emotions is correlated with the activation of certain areas of the brain, including the prefrontal cortex, a brain structure also associated with reasoning, strategizing, and reconciling competing concepts. When those parts of the brain associated with trust are active, critical analysis, logic, creative thinking, and verbal ability are more readily available to us.

By contrast, distrust is associated with increased levels of cortisol (a stress hormone) and adrenaline. It involves the amygdala, the part of the brain responsible in part for scanning the environment for and initiating reactions to threats. Emotions connected with distrust—such as anxiety, fear, and anger—are associated with lower-level brain and nervous-system processes initiated by the amygdala. In other words, the distrust network sets the brain on threat alert.

This network is designed to keep us safe. The decision to trust or not is based primarily on our emotional memory—how past experiences and the conditioning we got from our main caregivers have left us feeling about trusting versus distrusting. It operates below the level of conscious thought and is lightning fast relative to the higher-level thinking and reasoning of the trust network cortex.

Once we begin to distrust someone, we also start looking for confirming data—more reasons to distrust. This is called *confirmation bias*. We become suspicious, fearful, and defensive, or even offensive, toward the other person. Unchecked, the distrust network will do what it is intended to do. This process is good if trusting the other person poses a real danger. The problem is other people are seldom as threatening as the distrust network makes them out to be. We don't need to go into flight, fight, or freeze mode to protect ourselves. At the very least, we need to make a more objective assessment of the risks and rewards of trusting the other person.

The good news is the trust network has the capability to do just that. We can consciously intervene in the automatic nature of the distrust network and alter its directives. In other words, we can make conscious, intentional choices about trusting others that still take our emotional response into consideration but add higher-order thought to the process.

Building and maintaining trust involves activating the trust network and calming the distrust network in both ourselves and others. With intention, attention, and practice, we can moderate the neurophysiologic distrust response enough to take a step back and more objectively evaluate the situation. Intentionally using the distinctions of trust gives you a framework to use. Practicing good brain health habits, such as getting daily exercise and good sleep, eating a healthy diet, and meditating, will also support your ability to calm the distrust network and make a more objective assessment.[4]

Perhaps more importantly, knowledge of the trust distinctions and a basic understanding of the neurophysiology of trust and distrust together allow you to act in ways that have a far better chance of building and maintaining trusting relationships. If the ways you act can help the people around you feel fundamentally safe in your presence, they will also tend to trust you, feel a sense of well-being, and think, analyze, and problem solve at their best around you.

✅ TRUST CHECK

Read the following list of practices that are known to help people calm the brain's distrust network. Check the ones you currently do with some consistency:

- Get seven to eight hours of sleep per night.
- Exercise daily.
- Eat a healthy diet.
- Get at least twenty minutes of exposure to natural light every day.
- Have strong social connections.
- Meditate.
- Intentionally reflect on what you are grateful for at least once a day.
- Decide what one additional activity you would be willing to add to your daily routine.

CHAPTER 9

Trust and Team Success

A number of the executives characterized their years on the good-to-great teams as the high point of their lives.

—Jim Collins

I n most organizations the bulk of the work gets done through teams. Some groups, such as leadership teams, are ongoing, while other teams come together for a limited period of time to get something specific accomplished. No matter what their charter is, effective teams are the backbone of successful companies. And trust is always a key factor in the making of successful teams. But don't just take my word for it. Numerous studies confirm what most of us know from experience: strong trust is part of the fabric of high performing teams.[1]

But team trust is not a given. Like trust between two individuals, trust within a team is built and maintained over time through the actions and interactions of the team's members. The difference is multiple individuals are interacting on a team, so leaving trust-building practices to chance is even more perilous.

Distrust on a team is a performance killer just as it is between two people. But a team's goals are almost always larger and more influential for a company than those of any two individuals, so when a team's performance is hobbled by distrust, the fallout is far more damaging to the company. See table 2 for examples of common signs of high and low levels of trust within a team.

Table 2. Signs that teams have high or low trust

Common signs of high-trust teams	Common signs of low-trust teams
Team members use conflict productively.	Members avoid conflict or engage in destructive conflict.
Everyone is highly engaged with each other and the team's work.	Team members are disengaged.
People are committed to each other and the team's success.	Commitment to the team goals is low.
Members are accountable to each other and outside stakeholders.	Individuals avoid accountability.
Everyone develops innovative ideas and approaches.	Members lack innovation.
Members collaborate effectively.	Poor collaboration and a duplication of efforts occur.
Everyone is open, honest, and transparent.	People withhold information and have hidden agendas.
Team members get results and delight customers.	Deadlines are missed and output is poor.
True camaraderie exists throughout the team.	The team has false camaraderie, disinterest, and disrespect.

RAPHAEL'S LEADERSHIP TEAM

Raphael is a business unit vice president in a global company. He leads a team of nine people who are responsible for providing leadership for over one hundred employees scattered across four continents. Four members of his team work in the same location as Raphael; the other five are based in different geographic regions.

The concern Raphael initially expressed was that his team members were not collaborating well with each other. He recounted a number of instances in which individuals failed to share important information in a timely manner or didn't adequately support each other's initiatives in other ways. He wanted the team to, in his words, "act like a leadership team for the entire business unit and the company as a whole rather than a group of independent operators." He acknowledged some of the problem was structural in that the leaders' performance measures were specific only to their areas of responsibility. But Raphael felt something more fundamental was missing.

All the members of his team expressed strong trust in Raphael. But individual interviews with team members revealed generally low trust between them and strong distrust between certain individuals. One team member, for example, commented that he didn't ask fellow team members for advice or help because it didn't "feel safe" to reveal weaknesses they might exploit to their advantage. Many of them also complained about time wasted because people often failed to follow through on tasks they'd committed to doing. Some team members said they were afraid to openly disagree with some of the others on the team. Instead they would go to Raphael with their concerns.

Seeing the feedback, he realized it wasn't enough for him to trust and be trusted by each individual on his team. He also had to lead the way in fostering an environment where all of them could build and maintain strong trust with each other. When he looked at their behavior through the lens of the four assessments, he could see that the team needed to work to build trust in the domains of care, sincerity, and reliability. He also recognized it was up to him to lead the way. Over the course of about nine months, with the support of a coach, Raphael and his team were able to build the trust they needed. They became a high-trust team focused on their collective success. As a result, the entire business unit's performance increased substantially.

The actions and practices that build and maintain strong trust on teams include all of what has been covered so far. But some behaviors, actions, and practices are unique in building team trust, as Raphael and his team learned.

AGREE TO MAKE A SAFE ENVIRONMENT

Trusting, as we've said, requires making what you value vulnerable to others' actions. Much of what people value in themselves— their knowledge, expertise, creativity, passion, commitment, or self-respect—is exactly what their team needs from them. For people to be vulnerable to the team in this way requires a basic sense of safety. They need to believe what they contribute will be heard, respected, and considered. They need to know they will not be personally criticized, embarrassed, shamed, or shut down. They need to trust that their fellow team members have their individual good and the common interests of the team in mind. This assessment of trust in the domain of care underpins *psychological safety*, a condition first defined by Amy Edmondson.[2] In a famous study by Google, psychological safety was identified as the single most important factor in differentiating great performing teams from the merely good ones.[3]

When members of the team trust that they will not be attacked, embarrassed, shamed, or punished by their teammates or leader, they are willing to propose bold ideas, push to find the best solutions, listen to each other, express doubts or concerns, and ask for help from fellow team members when they need it. Establishing agreements about how team members will interact and treat each other is a powerful tool to begin creating a culture of care. Just having the conversation to develop and agree on team norms often serves to generate trust in the domain of care. Teams that review their norms regularly will deepen trust in both care and sincerity. People know they can trust each other when someone breaks a team norm, and another team member respectfully calls them on it. The act of establishing agreements and the practice of going over them regularly is usually part of a team leader's responsibility to the team.

Build Trust by Talking about It

Have a conversation about trust as a team. Identify what builds trust and what can damage it for each team member. Develop a short list of the critical behaviors and practices all team members—including the leader—can engage in to build it and behaviors that can damage it. Then commit as a team to doing or not doing what is on the list. It's also important to agree on how the team will handle it when a member does something they've agreed not to do. This kind of conversation is most useful when a team is newly forming, but it can be valuable to review at any time. One of the first steps Raphael took was to talk about trust with his team.

If trust is already reasonably high, this kind of conversation will feel easy and tend to focus on maintaining strong trust. On the other hand, if trust is low, talking about it will likely be difficult at first and could go in a bad direction if not handled well. In this case, engaging a skilled team coach or facilitator can be well worth the cost.

Consider All Voices

Research has shown that on high-trust, high-performance teams, all team members tend to spend a roughly equal amount of time speaking as they discuss possible actions and directions, make decisions, and coordinate action. When team members perceive their contributions are being listened to and considered by their teammates, trust builds in the domains of care and sincerity. This is something the team leader should make sure happens. But when everyone on the team takes responsibility to ensure every voice is heard, trust in the team as a whole is strengthened further.

Make and Use Team Agreements

Talk about and agree on how you will work with each other, including how you will work through disagreements and con-flicts; how decisions will be made; how you will make, keep, or change commitments (see chapter 4); what regular practices you will keep, such as starting each meeting with a quick check-in; how you will communicate with each other; and how you will hold each other accountable. Keeping team agreements—and addressing when the team, a team member, or the team leader fails to keep one of them—builds and strengthens trust in sincer-ity within the team. Review them regularly to make sure they are still relevant and being upheld.

Mind the Team's Charter

Along with reviewing team norms on a regular basis, keeping the team's charter front and center helps build trust in the domains of care, sincerity, and reliability. The charter or mission states the results the team is expected to produce for whom and why. It provides the context for all the conversations, decisions, and actions team members engage in together. It is the reason they exist as a team and defines the team's shared commitment to their stakeholders, including the company as a whole. The charter can be used as a guiding principle for the work the team takes on and decisions they make. It is also the ultimate context for requests and commitments team members make with one another and other stakeholders.

Foster Reliability

When team members consistently deliver on their commitments to each other, it ensures the team will deliver on its shared commitments to all other stakeholders. This generates trust at the individual and team level. Using the language of the Cycle of Commitment within the team leads to team members making trustworthy commitments to each other. Using the Cycle of Commitment with other stakeholders builds their trust in the team.

When a team fails to deliver, stakeholders will begin to distrust the team. This failure can be the result of several issues, including overpromising, failing to understand conditions of satisfaction, and failing to keep internal commitments. Being part of a distrusted team can taint every member's reputation within the company. Being on a highly trusted team, on the other hand, is good for the company, the team, and all its members.

Create Camaraderie

One of the most striking features of high-trust teams is the strong feeling of camaraderie among team members. They may disagree, argue, and debate passionately about the best course of action. But they do so as a band of comrades who in the end fully support the team's decisions. Throughout this process, they experience a high degree of joy in being with each other—something anyone who watches them in action can readily sense. They clearly trust and respect one another even when they disagree. They have fun with each other.

You might ask, Which comes first, trust or camaraderie? My experience is they build on each other over time as team members encounter each other at increasingly deeper levels of vulnerability and intimacy and experience repeatedly that each member does have the best interests of the others, the team, and the company at heart.

The conditions that support true camaraderie include the assessment by each team member that the others care for them and the team, the belief that each member brings value to the team, a willingness to challenge each other's thinking, the assessment that everyone on the team is honest and acts with integrity, faith in each other's competence and reliability, personal humility, and a sense of humor, including people's ability to laugh at themselves. As teams walk together through the fire of difficult conversations and hard decision-making with those conditions even partly in place, trust strengthens. As trust grows, so do those conditions that make for the kind of camaraderie that underlies stellar results.

THE FOUR DOMAINS OF TRUST FOR TEAMS

At the beginning of this book I defined four domains of trust. This framework offers individuals a way to think about both trusting other individuals wisely and behaving in ways that are worthy of others' trust. As I've worked with teams over the years, I have recast those four trust domains in a slightly different way for teams. Here are the ways teams think about themselves and act when there is trust among the team's members.

Care—We support each other's best interests and hold the team's interests above our own as individuals. We intend good for each other and assume positive intent. We are in this together.

Sincerity—We are transparent and honest and act with integrity as we work together. We act in good faith without hidden agendas.

Reliability—We consistently deliver on commitments we make to each other and to outside stakeholders. If we cannot deliver as promised, we let our customer know as soon as possible and renegotiate as necessary.

Competence—Each of has the skills, experience, and expertise needed to do what we are here to do. We expect team members to acknowledge when they need help and ask for it.

When a team takes time together to assess how they are doing in those four dimensions and then works on improving where they are falling short, trust grows stronger and the teams thrive.

PRACTICES FOR HIGH-TRUST TEAM LEADERSHIP

As Raphael's story illustrates, team leaders play a key role in building trust. A team's leader typically has more influence on a team than the other members. If you are a team leader, here are some steps you can take to facilitate strong team trust:

- Model trustworthy behavior. This may seem obvious, but leaders often forget that the people they lead are constantly looking to them for cues on how to behave. You need to show them the way when it comes to being trustworthy.
- Trust your team. It is equally important for you to trust your team. If you don't fully trust them, you need to lead the necessary conversations to build or repair trust.
- Ensure your team fully understands its charter—why it exists—and what it is expected to produce.
- Take the lead on defining team agreements and keeping them alive for the team.
- Be as transparent as you possibly can with everyone on the team. Avoid sharing certain information with only one or two team members unless it is absolutely necessary. If your team consists of some people you interact with regularly in person and others who are located remotely, make the extra time and effort to connect with those remote team members often. It will increase their trust in you and the team.
- Be clear about how team decisions will be made. Are you the final decision-maker? If so, what criteria will you use to make the decision? Will the team decide by consensus? Is one or a subset of the team members going to decide? Lack of clarity about the decision process often results in at least some team members distrusting the process, the people, or both.
- Address issues quickly. Whether one person exhibits a disruptive behavior, an interpersonal conflict flares up, or anything else distracts the team's attention from getting

☑ TRUST CHECK

Together as a team, have a conversation about the four domains of trust for teams.

- Have each team member rate the team as a group on how strong trust is in each of the four domains as described above. This can be done anonymously if it feels safer. Use a 1 to 7 scale, where 7 equals strong trust and 1 equals weak trust.
- If done anonymously, have one person read the results for each trust domain.
- Without identifying individuals, discuss at least two behaviors and actions that would increase the rating in each of the trust domains, even by one point on your scale.

Note that it may be best to have the support of a trained facilitator or coach for this kind of conversation, depending on the team's current level of trust.

good work done, it needs to be dealt with. These issues almost never go away by themselves. As team leader, you need to take the lead in addressing and resolving them.

- When a team's leader consciously and consistently acts in these ways, it creates an environment in which the team members find it easy to build and maintain trust with each other and repair it when it is damaged. It also forms the foundation for psychological safety.

CHAPTER 10

Putting It into Practice

The trust distinctions can be learned easily enough. Understanding and using the distinctions to act in ways that build trust and address and repair breakdowns in trust can become part of your way of being, unconsciously informing how you act at work and in all other areas of your life as well. The key is *practice*.

Here are some ways to begin:

- Start looking for the trust distinctions and their related behaviors in your interaction with coworkers.
- Stop and ask yourself, How am I acting in ways that build trust in my care, sincerity, reliability, and competence? What are others I trust saying and doing that makes them trustworthy? How do their actions relate to the four distinctions?
- As you become adept at observing through the lens of care, sincerity, reliability, and competence, begin asking yourself, what am I saying and doing that might be diminishing my trustworthiness in the eyes of others?
- Ask others whom you trust to tell you how they experience you in each of the four areas of trust.

- If you know you have difficulty with trustworthy behavior in a particular domain, tell others that you want to improve in this area, then clearly define what you will do differently and what you think the impact will be. Ask for regular feedback on how you're doing.
- Ask your direct reports, peers, or boss to tell you three actions you can start doing and three that you can stop doing to build even stronger trust with them.
- Have a conversation with someone you distrust. Express your concerns using the appropriate distinctions as a way to help both you and the other person feel safe even while you are having what may be an uncomfortable conversation.
- If you believe you may have betrayed the trust of someone who is important to you, ask them. If they tell you your behavior has caused them to question your trustworthiness, acknowledge it and apologize.

Building, maintaining, and restoring the trust of those you work with requires an understanding of how people assess trustworthiness, attention to your language and the actions related to the assessments you and others make about trust, and an intention to be a trusted leader, colleague, manager, and employee.

Building trust requires consistently behaving in ways others see as trustworthy and extending trust wisely. You now have a simple, powerful framework you can use to be effective at both. You have practices that will keep trust alive and well in your work relationships. Using the framework and practices presented in this book will greatly amplify all your strengths.

Relationships built on strong, healthy mutual trust are essential to both success and greater well-being in our companies, government, and social institutions as well as our communities and families.

Discussion Guide

The Thin Book of Trust

Over the years, I've heard from teams, companies, public agencies, school systems, churches, and other groups that have created their own questions for discussion and learning based on the material in this book. My intention for this discussion guide is to provide you with questions to spark inquiry, reflection, and learning so you don't have to invent them for yourself. Some of the questions below were even shared with me by groups like those listed above.

Feel free to choose those questions most relevant to your circumstances, whether you are answering them for your own learning or using them as a springboard for deeper study with a group of people.

I. TRUST IN THE DOMAIN OF CARE: SUPPORTING OTHERS' INTERESTS, TRUSTING THEY SUPPORT YOURS

Consider the following prompts regarding care in relation to trust:

- How important is it to you that the people you work with genuinely support you, have your best interests in mind, and intend good for you?

- What does it do for you when you trust that the people you work with hold your interests in mind and intend good for you?
- What is the cost of not having or questioning that trust?
- Write a list of the behaviors and actions you look for in others that allow you to assess to what extent you can trust them in the domain of care. Put them in order of importance to you. What do you notice?
- Would your list differ between people and in different situations? Why or why not?
- How consistently do you demonstrate the behaviors and actions on your list toward others?
- What assumptions do you have about how people assess your trustworthiness in this domain?
- How can you check these assumptions?

II. TRUST IN THE DOMAIN OF SINCERITY: WORKING WITH HONESTY AND INTEGRITY

Bring to mind someone you consider to be highly trustworthy in this domain, and consider the following questions:

- What does trusting this person's sincerity make possible for you? If you work with this person, how does trusting they are sincere benefit you and others with whom you work?
- What is the cost of distrusting or questioning the sincerity of people you work with?
- What is the cost if others distrust or question your sincerity?
- What does being honest mean to you in practice?

- What standard of honesty do you hold others to? Do they know what your standard is?
- What standard do you hold yourself to?
- What does meeting this standard of honesty require of you and the people you work with?
- What does integrity look and sound like in others? What does acting with integrity feel like for you?
- What are your expectations for honesty and integrity in the following people: your boss, people who report to you, your peers, teams you are part of, your organization's senior leadership, and yourself?
- Do your expectations differ between people or in different circumstances? If so, how and why?

III. TRUST IN THE DOMAIN OF RELIABILITY: MAKING AND FULFILLING COMMITMENTS

Imagine a one-to-one work relationship or team in which all parties can fully rely on each other to fulfill the commitments they make or, if something comes up and they can't, can say so right away. The reality is that distrust resulting from unfulfilled or poorly fulfilled commitments is the most common trust issue for managers and teams. What could change this for you and others in your workplace? The simplest, most effective way to change this is to use the Cycle of Commitment as described in chapter 4. Below are some discussion prompts focused on the cycle:

- Write about a request you recently made to someone that was not fulfilled to your satisfaction (e.g., not completed on time, what happened was not what you expected).

- Go to the section in chapter 4 that talks about clear and complete requests, and check to see how clear and complete that request was. What was missing?
- Does the completeness of your requests change in different circumstances? If so, how and under what circumstances?
- What channels do you use to make requests in your workplace: for example, in person, phone, voicemail, email, text, instant messaging, or Slack. Which are most and least effective? Which ones do you use most often?
- How often do you make drive-by requests—that is, you don't wait for a response from the intended performer? To whom do you make such requests? Making drive-by requests is very easy on asynchronous communication channels, such as email and text.
- To what extent do people you work with hold each other accountable for commitments not fulfilled?
- What do you do when someone fails to fully deliver on a commitment to you?
- Do people in your workplace consistently hold each other accountable? If so, how?
- How often do you say yes to requests without first determining you actually have the capacity to deliver? What is the impact on you and others you work with when you do this?
- Are there certain people you blindly say yes to? Who are they? Why do you do it?
- Do you say no or make a counteroffer when you know you cannot do what someone is asking of you?
- Are there circumstances in which you believe you can't say no? If you can't say no, how can you declare a trustworthy yes?

IV. TRUST IN THE DOMAIN OF COMPETENCE: ABILITY TO DO WHAT'S EXPECTED

Take a few moments to assess what your current role requires of you in terms of experience, expertise, knowledge, and capabilities. These might include technical expertise, managerial know-how, leadership ability, emotional intelligence, discernment, grace under fire, or ability to motivate others. Then ask yourself the following questions:

- What standards do you hold yourself to for each of these skills and competencies?
- Are your standards the same as those of your boss, your peers, your employees, and other stakeholders? How do you know?
- What standards do you hold others to? Are they aware of the standards you are expecting them to meet?
- What skills and competencies could you add that would allow you to be more effective at your job?
- Do you seek feedback from others to help you determine where you are fully competent and what you might need to get better at? Whom do you ask for this feedback?
- What do you do when you recognize you are not fully competent in some aspect of your job?
- To what extent are you comfortable acknowledging a lack of competence and asking for help?

Notes

CHAPTER 3

1. Peter M. Senge, Art Kleiner, Charlotte Roberts, Richard B. Ross, and Bryan J. Smith, *The Fifth Discipline Fieldbook: Strategies and Tools for Building a Learning Organization* (New York: Doubleday, 1994), 246–250. This exercise was originally developed by Chris Argyris and Donald A. Schön and first presented in their book *Theory in Practice: Increasing Professional Effectiveness* (San Francisco: Jossey-Bass, 1974).

CHAPTER 4

1. A number of thinkers, authors, and teachers have contributed to the understanding of requests, offers, and promises as critical to getting good work done, maintaining trust, and increasing well-being. Key among them are Robert Dunham, Julio Olalla, Rafael Echeverria, and Richard LeKander. See also Terry Winograd and Fernando Flores, *Understanding Computers and Cognition: A New Foundation for Design* (Reading, MA: Addison-Wesley Professional, 1987).
2. Geert Hofstede and Gert Jan Hofstede, *Culture and Organizations: Software of the Mind* (New York: McGraw-Hill, 2005).

CHAPTER 6

1. Tony Simons, "The High Cost of Lost Trust," *Harvard Business Review*, September 2002.
2. See, for example, T. R. Tyler and P. Degoey, "Trust in Organizational Authorities: The Influence of Motive Attributions on Willingness to Accept Decisions," in *Trust in Organizations: Frontiers of Theory and Research*, ed. R. M. Kramer and T. R. Tyler (Thousand Oaks, CA: Sage Publications, 1996), 331–356. See also S. L. Robinson, "Trust

and Breach of the Psychological Contract," *Administrative Science Quarterly* 41, no. 4 (December 1996): 574–599.

3. Robert C. Solomon and Fernando Flores, *Building Trust in Business, Politics, Relationships and Life* (Oxford: Oxford University Press, 2001), 11.

4. Michael Wilkinson has a paper entitled "Why Don't You Trust Me: The Five Cs of Trust" available on the Leadership Strategies website with another useful example of initiating trust conversations. His opening and the one suggested in this book are similar. For more information, visit www.leadstrat.com.

CHAPTER 8

1. See, for example, Angelika Dimoka, "What Does the Brain Tell Us about Trust and Distrust? Evidence from a Functional Neuroimaging Study," *MIS Quarterly* 34, no. 2 (June 2010): 373–396.

2. Eveline van Zeeland-van der Holst and Jörg Henseler, "Thinking outside the Box: A Neuroscientific Perspective on Trust in B2B Relationships," *IMP Journal* 12, no. 1 (March 2018): 75–110.

3. K. Uvnas-Moberg, "Oxytocin May Mediate the Benefits of Positive Social Interaction and Emotions," *Psychoneuroendocrinology* 23, no. 8 (November 1998): 819–835; and Peter Kirsch et al., "Oxytocin Modulates Neural Circuitry for Social Cognition and Fear in Humans," *Journal of Neuroscience* 25, no. 49 (December 2005): 11489–11493.

4. David Rock, *Your Brain at Work: Strategies for Overcoming Distraction, Regaining Focus, and Working Smarter All Day Long*, rev. ed. (New York: Harper Business, 2020).

CHAPTER 9

1. Bart de Jong, Kurt Dirks, and Nichole Gillespie, "Trust and Team Performance: A Meta-Analysis of Main Effects, Moderators and Covariates," *Journal of Applied Psychology* 101, no. 8 (April 2016).

2. Amy C. Edmondson, "Psychological Safety, Trust, and Learning in Organizations: A Group-Level Lens," in *Trust and Distrust in Organizations: Dilemmas and Approaches*, ed. Roderick Kramer and Karen Cook (New York: Russell Sage Foundation, 2004), 239–272.

3. Charles Duhigg, "What Google Learned from Its Quest to Build the Perfect Team," *New York Times Magazine*, February 25, 2016.

Trust at Work Field Guide

The Trust at Work Field Guide is a companion to *The Thin Book of Trust*. In it you will find additional trust-building examples, exercises, and practices to support building and sustaining trust one on one, as well as creating a high-trust culture in teams and other groups at work.

The Trust at Work Field Guide is a free PDF document provided by Insight Coaching. You can access it using this QR code or by visiting insightcoaching.com/trust-at-work-field-guide/.

Acknowledgments

There are no new ideas in this book; I can claim only their unique arrangement and expression. I would like to acknowledge several people whose thinking on trust contributed to this volume. First, my coaching clients, from whom I continue to learn much about the difficulties and rewards of building and maintaining strong trust in the workplace.

Julio Olalla, teacher, lecturer, and founder of the Newfield Network. I first understood the power of separating trust into distinct but interlocking assessments from Julio's teachings.

Tony Simons of Cornell University, who first introduced me to the large body of academic research on trust that continues to expand my understanding of the topic.

The many fellow coaches, consultants, and facilitators from whom I am constantly learning about how to support building trust in the workplace, including Ila Edgar, Amanda Blake, Newell Eaton, Mark Robertson, Nancy Settle-Murphy, and the growing number of Trust at Work Certification Program alumni, to name just a few.

Index

About the Author

For over twenty-five years, Charles Feltman has been serving people who are seeking to develop themselves into the leaders they want and need to be to meet the challenges they have chosen for themselves. As an executive and team coach, and through leadership development programs, Charles has supported his clients in increasing success and well-being for themselves and the people they lead. His clients are executives, other senior leaders, and leadership teams in companies of all sizes and sectors across multiple industries, including tech, manufacturing, service, education, government, and NGOs. His work has often included supporting individuals, teams, and entire organizations in becoming exceptional at building and maintaining strong trust as a foundation for achieving their mission and vision.

Berrett–Koehler
Publishers

Berrett-Koehler is an independent publisher dedicated to an ambitious mission: *Connecting people and ideas to create a world that works for all.*

Our publications span many formats, including print, digital, audio, and video. We also offer online resources, training, and gatherings. And we will continue expanding our products and services to advance our mission.

We believe that the solutions to the world's problems will come from all of us, working at all levels: in our society, in our organizations, and in our own lives. Our publications and resources offer pathways to creating a more just, equitable, and sustainable society. They help people make their organizations more humane, democratic, diverse, and effective (and we don't think there's any contradiction there). And they guide people in creating positive change in their own lives and aligning their personal practices with their aspirations for a better world.

And we strive to practice what we preach through what we call "The BK Way." At the core of this approach is *stewardship,* a deep sense of responsibility to administer the company for the benefit of all of our stakeholder groups, including authors, customers, employees, investors, service providers, sales partners, and the communities and environment around us. Everything we do is built around stewardship and our other core values of *quality, partnership, inclusion,* and *sustainability.*

This is why Berrett-Koehler is the first book publishing company to be both a B Corporation (a rigorous certification) and a benefit corporation (a for-profit legal status), which together require us to adhere to the highest standards for corporate, social, and environmental performance. And it is why we have instituted many pioneering practices (which you can learn about at www.bkconnection.com), including the Berrett-Koehler Constitution, the Bill of Rights and Responsibilities for BK Authors, and our unique Author Days.

We are grateful to our readers, authors, and other friends who are supporting our mission. We ask you to share with us examples of how BK publications and resources are making a difference in your lives, organizations, and communities at www.bkconnection.com/impact.

Dear reader,

Thank you for picking up this book and welcome to the worldwide BK community! You're joining a special group of people who have come together to create positive change in their lives, organizations, and communities.

What's BK all about?

Our mission is to connect people and ideas to create a world that works for all.

Why? Our communities, organizations, and lives get bogged down by old paradigms of self-interest, exclusion, hierarchy, and privilege. But we believe that can change. That's why we seek the leading experts on these challenges—and share their actionable ideas with you.

A welcome gift

To help you get started, we'd like to offer you a **free copy** of one of our bestselling ebooks:

www.bkconnection.com/welcome

When you claim your **free ebook**, you'll also be subscribed to our blog.

Our freshest insights

Access the best new tools and ideas for leaders at all levels on our blog at ideas.bkconnection.com.

Sincerely,

Your friends at Berrett-Koehler

Certified

Corporation